MS Office 95
one step at a time

BOOKS AVAILABLE

By both authors:

MS Office 95
one step at a time

by

N. Kantaris
and
P.R.M. Oliver

BERNARD BABANI (publishing) LTD
THE GRAMPIANS
SHEPHERDS BUSH ROAD
LONDON W6 7NF
ENGLAND

PLEASE NOTE

Although every care has been taken with the production of this book to ensure that any projects, designs, modifications and/or programs, etc., contained herewith, operate in a correct and safe manner and also that any components specified are normally available in Great Britain, the Publishers and Author(s) do not accept responsibility in any way for the failure (including fault in design) of any project, design, modification or program to work correctly or to cause damage to any equipment that it may be connected to or used in conjunction with, or in respect of any other damage or injury that may be so caused, nor do the Publishers accept responsibility in any way for the failure to obtain specified components.

Notice is also given that if equipment that is still under warranty is modified in any way or used or connected with home-built equipment then that warranty may be void.

© 1996 BERNARD BABANI (publishing) LTD

First Published - May 1996
Reprinted - March 1997

British Library Cataloguing in Publication Data

A catalogue record for this book is available from the British Library

ISBN 0 85934 409 6

Cover Design by Gregor Arthur
Cover illustrations by Adam Wills
Printed and Bound in Great Britain by Cox & Wyman Ltd, Reading

ABOUT THIS BOOK

MS Office 95 one step at a time has been written to help users to get to grips with the integrated components of this package, namely, the word processor *Word 7*, the spreadsheet *Excel 7*, and the presentation graphics *PowerPoint* 7. All these components were specifically written for *Windows 95*. If you have *MS Office Pro*, the package should include the database *Access 7*. If it doesn't, contact your supplier for a free upgrade to *Access 7*.

The book does not describe how to install and use Microsoft Windows 95. If you need to know more about the Windows environment, then we suggest you select an appropriate level book for your needs from the 'Books Available' list - the books are graduated in complexity with the less demanding *One step at a time* series, to the more detailed *Explained* series. They are all published by BERNARD BABANI (publishing) Ltd.

The individual applications which make up Microsoft Office are designed to work together and have the same look and feel, which makes it easy to learn. For example, the majority of menus, toolbar buttons, and dialogue boxes are the same in each application, which gives them a consistent interface, and makes it easier to share information between them.

The package improves on previous Office capabilities, such as the ability to

- create a document in Word, and then embed a chart or a worksheet from Excel in the Word document,

- create a link between Word and a chart or worksheet in Excel so that when you change the data in Excel, the Word document is updated automatically,

- insert an Excel worksheet into a PowerPoint slide so that you can display it during a presentation.

Below we list some of the new features to this latest version of Microsoft Office:

- The Answer Wizard; a natural language interface to the Help system.

- An Office Binder, enabling the production of multi-application documents.

- Improved IntelliSense features which help you with your work.

- Add-ins which allow Word to be used as an e-mail front-end and Internet browser.

- An intelligent Wizard which allows you to convert spreadsheets into Access databases.

- The addition of contact management capabilities to Schedule+.

- More use of Wizards throughout the package and improved workgroup capabilities.

As you can see, the various applications within Microsoft Office can either be used by themselves or made to share information. This book introduces each application by itself, with sufficient detail to get you working, then discusses how to share information between them. No prior knowledge of these packages is assumed.

The book was written with the busy person in mind. It is not necessary to learn all there is to know about a subject, when reading a few selected pages can usually do the same thing quite adequately. With the help of this book, it is hoped that you will be able to come to terms with Microsoft Office and get the most out of your computer in terms of efficiency, productivity and enjoyment, and that you will be able to do it in the shortest, most effective and informative way.

If you would like to purchase a Companion Disc for any of the listed books by the same author(s), apart from the ones marked with an asterisk, containing the file/program listings which appear in them, then fill in the form at the back of the book and send it to Phil Oliver at the stipulated address.

ABOUT THE AUTHORS

Noel Kantaris graduated in Electrical Engineering at Bristol University and after spending three years in the Electronics Industry in London, took up a Tutorship in Physics at the University of Queensland. Research interests in Ionospheric Physics, led to the degrees of M.E. in Electronics and Ph.D. in Physics. On return to the UK, he took up a Post-Doctoral Research Fellowship in Radio Physics at the University of Leicester, and then in 1973 a lecturing position in Engineering at the Camborne School of Mines, Cornwall, (part of Exeter University), where since 1978 he has also assumed the responsibility for the Computing Department.

Phil Oliver graduated in Mining Engineering at Camborne School of Mines in 1967 and since then has specialised in most aspects of surface mining technology, with a particular emphasis on computer related techniques. He has worked in Guyana, Canada, several Middle Eastern countries, South Africa and the United Kingdom, on such diverse projects as: the planning and management of bauxite, iron, gold and coal mines; rock excavation contracting in the UK; international mining equipment sales and international mine consulting for a major mining house in South Africa. In 1988 he took up a lecturing position at Camborne School of Mines (part of Exeter University) in Surface Mining and Management.

ACKNOWLEDGEMENTS

We would like to thank the staff of Text 100 Limited for providing the software programs on which this work was based. We would also like to thank colleagues at the Camborne School of Mines for the helpful tips and suggestions which assisted us in the writing of this book.

TRADEMARKS

CONTENTS

1. PACKAGE OVERVIEW

Microsoft Office 95 is a collection of full-featured products with the same look and feel that work together as if they were a single program.

Microsoft Office 95 includes Microsoft Word, Excel, and PowerPoint. The Professional version of Microsoft Office 95 also includes the fully relational database management system Access. With both versions of MS Office 95 you also get Schedule+ which allows you to schedule your time and contacts. All Office 95 applications have a built-in consistency which makes them easier to use. For example, all applications in MS Office 95 have standardised toolbars and consistent menus, commands, and dialogue boxes. Once you become familiar with one application, it is far easier to learn and use the others.

All MS Office 95 applications make use of what is known as IntelliSense, which anticipates what you want to do and produces the correct result. For example, AutoCorrect and AutoFormat in Word can, when activated, correct common spelling mistakes and format an entire document automatically, while TipWizard in Excel can give you hints on how to work faster and more efficiently. Other Wizards in all four applications can help you with everyday tasks and/or make complex tasks easier to manage.

With OfficeLinks and OLE (Object Linking and Embedding), you can move and share information seamlessly between MS Office 95 applications. For example, you can drag information from one application to another, and can insert a Microsoft Excel worksheet directly into a Word document by simply clicking a button on a Word toolbar.

Finally, Microsoft Visual Basic for Applications, gives you a powerful and flexible development platform with which to create custom solutions.

Hardware and Software Requirements

If Microsoft Office is already installed on your computer, you can safely skip the rest of this chapter.

To install and use MS Office, you need an IBM-compatible PC equipped with Intel's 80386sx (or higher) processor. We recommend a minimum processor speed of 33 megahertz (MHz). In addition, you need the following:

- Windows 95, Windows NT or Windows NT Advanced Server version.

- Random access memory (RAM): 4MB; 8MB recommended when running multiple programs.

- Hard disc space available for MS Office 95 Standard: 28MB for compact installation; 55MB for typical; 89MB for custom. For MS Office 95 Professional: 42MB for compact; 72MB for typical; 117MB for custom.

- Video adapter: VGA or higher resolution. If you are using PowerPoint, you will need a 256-colour video adapter.

- Pointing device: Microsoft Mouse or compatible.

Realistically, to run MS Office Pro with reasonable sized applications, you will need a 486 or a Pentium PC with at least 8MB of RAM. To run Microsoft Office 95 from a network, you must also have a network compatible with your Windows operating environment, such as Microsoft's Windows 95, Windows NT, LAN Manager, or Novell's NetWare.

To use Microsoft Mail, you must acquire the server version of Microsoft Mail for PC Networks, even though MS Office includes a client licence. The software required to run Microsoft Mail is included with the server version which must be ordered separately.

Installing MS OFFICE 95

Installing MS Office on your computer's hard disc is made very easy with the use of the SETUP program, which even configures MS Office automatically to take advantage of the computer's hardware. One of SETUP's functions is to convert compressed Office files from the distribution discs, or CD-ROM, prior to copying them onto your hard disc.

Note: If you are using a virus detection utility, disable it before running SETUP, as it might conflict with it.

To install MS Office, click the **Start** button and select the **Run** command, as shown below left. Selecting this command, opens the Run dialogue box, as shown below right.

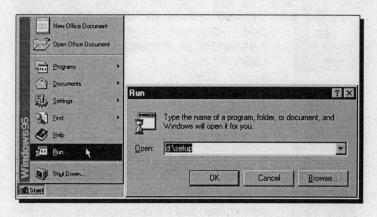

If the application was distributed on diskettes, insert disc #1 into the A: drive and type in the **Command Line** box:

```
a:\setup
```

In our case we used the CD-ROM in the D: drive. Clicking the **OK** button, starts the installation of Microsoft Office 95. SETUP does the following:

- Asks you to close any open applications.

- Prompts you to type your name and the name of your organisation (optional).

- Prompts you to write down the product ID number on your registration card.

- Prompts you to supply the path to the directory where you want to install Office, and then checks your system and the available hard disc space.

Next, select the type of installation you want. The SETUP program provides four basic options. The available options vary depending on how you are installing Office; directly from discs or CD-ROM, or from the network.

 Typical installs all Office applications and popular components. This installation is recommended for most users.

 Compact lets you install all of the Office applications. This installation is recommended for systems with minimum hard disc space.

 Custom includes **Typical** installation and the option to add or remove components. This installation is recommended for power users.

 Run from CD-ROM is only available if you are setting up Office from a CD-ROM. Shared components are installed on the hard disc.

Obviously, depending on the type of set-up, some options may not be available. We selected the **Custom** option.

4

If you select the **Custom** installation, the following is displayed:

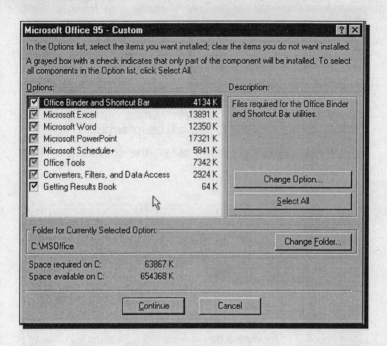

Make sure the check boxes next to the application or component names are selected for all items that you want to install. A selected item displays a "√" in its check box. If you do not want to install an application or component, make sure that its check box is cleared by clicking it. To install all of the applications and all of their components, choose the **Continue** button.

To install part of an application or component, highlight its name by clicking it, then click the **Change Option** button. Clear the check boxes for any options you don't want to install, and then choose the **OK** button. When you finish, choose the **Continue** button.

Depending on the options you select, you may need to respond to additional prompts.

Finally, SETUP asks you to select the paper format and language, before starting to transfer files to your hard disc. Throughout installation SETUP informs you on what it is doing and what percentage of the total file transfer it has covered, as shown above. Once installation is completed successfully, you will be informed.

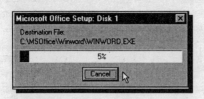

When you restart your computer, the following screen is displayed.

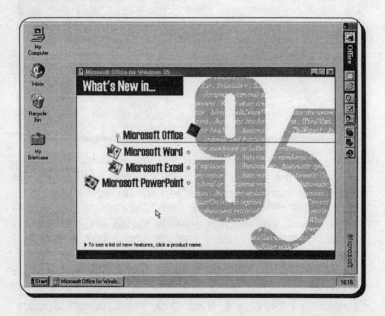

During set-up, the Microsoft Shortcut Bar is added to the Windows 95 StartUp program so that it will be displayed automatically to the right of your screen whenever you start your system.

In the What's New ... screen of the Standard Office version, there are four options to choose from. With the Professional version of Office you will also have the option of finding out what is new in Access. We suggest you look through the applications you intend to use, but if you need to come back to this screen, then click the Answer Wizard icon on the Office Shortcut Bar, shown here, and type in the **Type your request** box *Microsoft Office*, then click the **S̲earch** button and double-click the *What's new in Microsoft Office 95* in the **Se̲lect a topic** box in the **Tell me About** list.

Adding or Removing Office Applications:

To add or remove an Office application

* Close all open applications, including the Office Shortcut Bar. To do the latter, left-click the area with the small button at the top of the Office Shortcut Bar, shown here, then click the **Ex̲it** option.

* Point to **S̲ettings** on the Windows **Start** menu, and click Control Panel. Next, double-click the Add/Remove Programs icon, shown here, and then click the Install/Uninstall tab. Click the Microsoft Office application, and then click **Add/R̲emove**.

* Follow the instructions on the screen.

To recover the Office Shortcut Bar, click **Start**, select **Find, Files or Folders**, and type *Shortcut* in the **Named** box. Double-clicking the first of the three found files, restores the Office Shortcut Bar.

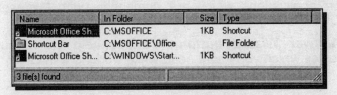

Name	In Folder	Size	Type
Microsoft Office Sh...	C:\MSOFFICE	1KB	Shortcut
Shortcut Bar	C:\MSOFFICE\Office		File Folder
Microsoft Office Sh...	C:\WINDOWS\Start...	1KB	Shortcut

3 file(s) found

The Office Shortcut Bar

The Microsoft Office Shortcut Bar, provides a convenient way to work with your documents and the Office applications by complementing the Windows 95 **Start** menu.

The various icons on the Shortcut Bar, shown below, have the following function:

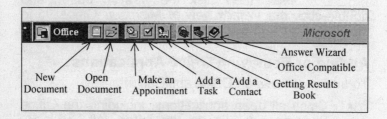

The Start a New Document button: Allows you to select in the displayed dialogue box the tab containing the type of document you want to work with. Double-clicking the type of document or template you want, automatically loads the appropriate application.

The Open a Document button: Allows you to work with an existing document. Opening a document, first starts the application originally used to create it.

The Schedule buttons: Allow you to schedule an appointment, schedule a task, and add a contact name.

Getting Results Book button: Provides you with suggestions on how to work efficiently with the Microsoft Office applications.

Office Compatible button: Provides demonstrations on applications which are compatible with Microsoft Office.

Answer Wizard button: Provides help on various topics which you might need while working with Office.

Changing the Office Shortcut Bar:

You have the option of changing the buttons on the Office Shortcut Bar. To do so, left-click on an empty part of the Shortcut bar to display the available options, as shown at the bottom below.

Of these, we find the 'Old Office' option the most useful. Clicking this option, replaces the original Office Shortcut Bar with the one shown here. However, clicking the Office icon (top left), changes the Shortcut Bar back to the original Office and places the Old Office icon (bottom left) at the extreme bottom of the Bar. You can then flick between the two by clicking the appropriate icon. The function of the various buttons on the Old Office Shortcut Bar are as shown on the right.

Adding/Deleting Buttons:

You can add buttons to the Shortcut Bar by dragging them there. To find the application you want to add to the Shortcut Bar, click the **Start** button and use **Find**.

To delete a button, right-click on an empty part of the Shortcut Bar, select **Customize** from the displayed menu, then click the Buttons tab, select the unwanted button and click **Delete**. But beware, this also deletes the folder that holds the application! It may be better to hide it.

Old Office

MS-Word
MS-Excel
PowerPoint
MS-DOS Prompt
Schedule+
MS-Mail
Explorer
Notepad
MS-Paint
Calculator
MS-Access

✔ Office
Favorites
✔ Old Office
Desktop
MSN
Programs
Accessories

Auto Hide
Customize...
Refresh Icons

Hiding/Displaying Buttons:

To hide a button from the Shortcut Bar (without deleting it), right-click on the button and select the **Hide Button** option on the displayed menu, shown here.

To display previously hidden buttons, right-click the Shortcut Bar, use the **Customize** option, on the displayed menu and click the Button tab. Clicking on the check box of the required button makes it visible on the Shortcut Bar. Clicking again, clears its check mark and hides it.

The Mouse Pointers

In MS Office applications, as with all other graphical based programs, the use of a mouse makes many operations both easier and more fun to carry out.

MS Office makes use of the mouse pointers available in Windows 95, some of the most common of which are illustrated below. When an MS Office application is initially started up the first you will see is the hourglass, which turns into an upward pointing hollow arrow once the individual application screen appears on your display. Other shapes depend on the type of work you are doing at the time.

 The hourglass which displays when you are waiting while performing a function.

 The arrow which appears when the pointer is placed over menus, scrolling bars, and buttons.

I The I-beam which appears in normal text areas of the screen.

⬧ The large 4-headed arrow which appears after choosing the **Control, Move/Size** command(s) for moving or sizing windows.

↔ The double arrows which appear when over the border of a window, used to drag the side and alter the size of the window.

🖑 The Help hand which appears in the Help windows, and is used to access 'hypertext' type links.

MS Office applications, like other Windows packages, have additional mouse pointers which facilitate the execution of selected commands. Some of these are:

↓ The vertical pointer which appears when pointing over a column in a table or worksheet and used to select the column.

➡ The horizontal pointer which appears when pointing at a row in a table or worksheet and used to select the row.

⇗ The slanted arrow which appears when the pointer is placed in the selection bar area of text or a table.

◄‖► The vertical split arrow which appears when pointing over the area separating two columns and used to size a column.

⬍ The horizontal split arrow which appears when pointing over the area separating two rows and used to size a row.

+ The frame cross which you drag to create a frame.

✏ The draw pointer which appears when you are drawing freehand.

Some applications display a '?' button on the right end of their title bar, as shown here. Clicking this button changes the mouse pointer from its usual inclined arrow shape to the 'What's this?' shape. Pointing to an object in the window and clicking, opens a Help topic.

MS Office has a few additional mouse pointers to the ones above, but their shape is mostly self-evident.

2. WORD PROCESSING WITH WORD

Starting the Program

Word is started in Windows 95 either by clicking the **Start** button then selecting **Program** and clicking on the 'Microsoft Word' icon on the cascade menu, clicking the Word icon on the Old Office Shortcut Bar, or by clicking the 'Open a Document' icon on the Office Shortcut Bar and double-clicking on a Word document file. In the latter case the document will be loaded into Word at the same time.

The first time you use Word you get the 'What' New' Help screen displayed. After that, to get back to this Help screen, use **Help, Answer Wizard** and type *what's new* in the Type Your Request box, then select What's New in Microsoft Word 95. We suggest you spend a little time examining at least the first three options of this Help screen.

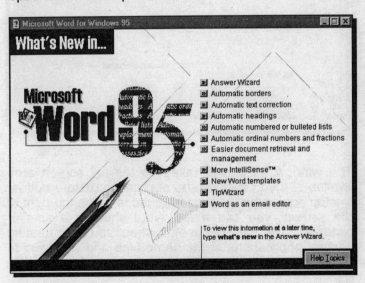

The Word Screen

The opening 'blank' screen of Word for Windows 95 is shown below. It is perhaps worth spending some time looking at the various parts that make up this screen. Word follows the usual Microsoft Windows 95 conventions and if you are familiar with these you can skip through this section. Otherwise a few minutes might be well spent here.

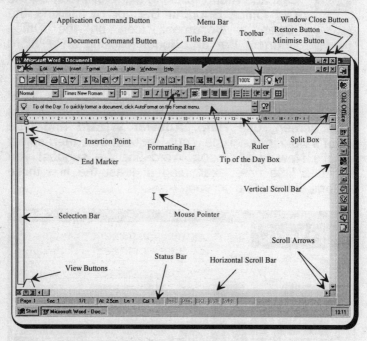

The window as shown takes up the full screen area available. If you click on the application restore button, the top one of the two restore buttons at the top right of the screen, you can make Word show in a smaller window. This can be useful when you are running several applications at the same time and you want to transfer between them with the mouse.

Note that the Word window, which in this case displays an empty document with the title 'Document1', has a solid 'Title bar', indicating that it is the active application window. Although multiple windows can be displayed simultaneously, you can only enter data into the active window (which will always be displayed on top). Title bars of non active windows appear a lighter shade than that of the active one.

The Word screen is divided into several areas which have the following functions:

Area	*Function*
Command buttons	Clicking on the top command button, (see upper-left corner of the Word window), displays a pull-down menu which can be used to control the program window. It includes commands for restoring, moving, sizing, maximising, minimising, and closing the window. The lower command button controls the current document window in the same manner.
Title Bar	The bar at the top of a window which displays the application name and the name of the current document.
Minimise Button	When clicked on, this button minimises the application to the Windows Taskbar, or a document to an icon.
Restore Button	When clicked on, this button restores the active window to the position and size that

was occupied before it was maximised. The restore button is then replaced by a Maximise button, as shown here, which is used to set the window to full screen size.

Close button
: The extreme top right button that you click to close a window.

Menu Bar
: The bar below the Title bar which allows you to choose from several menu options. Clicking on a menu item displays the pull-down menu associated with that item.

Toolbar
: The bar below the Menu bar which contains buttons that give you mouse click access to the functions most often used in the program. These are grouped according to function.

Formatting Bar
: The buttons on the Formatting Bar allow you to change the attributes of a font, such as italic and underline, and also to format text in various ways. The Formatting Bar contains three boxes; a style box, a font box and a size box which show which style, font and size of characters are currently being used. These boxes give access to other installed styles, fonts and character sizes.

Ruler
: The area where you can see and set tabulation points and indents.

Split Box	The area above the top vertical scroll button which when dragged allows you to split the screen.
Scroll Bars	The areas on the screen (extreme right and bottom of each window) that contain scroll boxes in vertical and horizontal bars. Clicking on these bars allows you to control the part of a document which is visible on the screen.
Scroll Arrows	The arrowheads at each end of each scroll bar at which you can click to scroll the screen up and down one line, or left and right 10% of the screen, at a time.
Selection Bar	The area on the screen in the left margin of the Word window (marked here with a box for convenience), where the mouse pointer changes to an arrow that slants to the right. Clicking the left mouse button once selects the current line, while clicking twice selects the current paragraph.
Insertion pointer	The pointer used to specify the place of text insertion.
Views Buttons	Clicking these buttons changes screen views quickly.
Status Bar	The bottom line of the document window that displays status information, and in which a short help description appears when you point and click on a button.

The Formatting Bar:

This is located below the Toolbar at the top of the Word for Windows screen and is divided into seven sections, as shown below. These can only be accessed by clicking on them with the left mouse button.

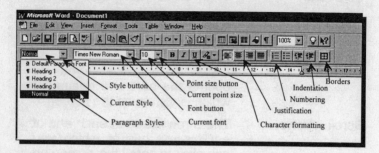

The Current Style box on the left of the Character formatting buttons, shows the style of the current paragraph; the one containing the cursor. By clicking the down-arrow button next to it, a list of all the available styles in the active template is produced (as shown). Clicking on one of these will change the style of the current paragraph.

To the right of the Style button is the Current font box which shows the current typeface. Clicking on the down-arrow button to the right of it allows you to change the typeface of any selected text. The Current point size box shows the size of selected characters. This size can be changed by clicking on the down-arrow button next to it and selecting another size from the displayed list.

Next, are four Character formatting buttons which allow you to enhance selected text by emboldening, italicising, underlining, or colour highlighting it. The next four buttons allow you to change the justification of a selected paragraph, and the next four help you set the different types of Numbering and Indentation options. The last button allows you to add borders and shading to selected paragraphs, table cells and frames.

The Status Bar:

This is located at the bottom of the Word window and is used to display statistics about the active document.

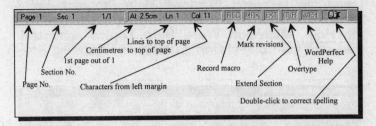

For example, when a document is being opened, the Status bar displays for a short time its name and length in terms of total number of characters. Once a document is opened, the Status bar displays the statistics of the document at the insertion point; here it is on Page 1, Section 1, 11 characters from the left margin. Double-clicking the left of the status bar displays the Go To dialogue box, and double-clicking the other features will activate them. There is even help for WordPerfect users converting to Word. To activate this facility, double-click on **WPH**, or to make it 'permanent' use the **Help** command, select **WordPerfect Help,** click the **Options** button in the displayed dialogue box, and check the **Help for WordPerfect Users** box.

Note: If you do not need to have the **Help for WordPerfect Users** permanently available to you, it is a good idea not to set this option as it can have an adverse effect on the way you work. For example, if the WordPerfect Users help is switched on, you cannot delete sections of your document by highlighting them and pressing the <Del> key. We find this extremely annoying. Another annoying feature we found is that you will have to specify hanging indents separately for each paragraph without being able to carry the formatting from the first paragraph to the rest by simply pressing the <Enter> key. The list does not end with these two examples; there are many more!

Using Help in Word

Using the Microsoft Windows Help Program, Word provides on-line Help for every function. You can use the **Help, Microsoft Word Help Topics** command, then click the Contents tab, to obtain the following:

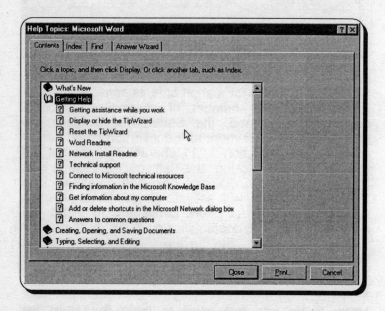

Help topics can be printed on paper by selecting the topic, then clicking the **Print** button.

Another way of obtaining help on a specific topic is to select the Answer Wizard, either by clicking its tab on the above window, or selecting it from the **Help** menu, then typing the request in the top box, as follows:

Pressing the **Search** button, lists the following information in the second box:

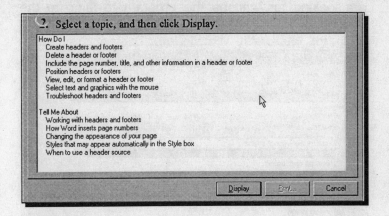

In addition, there are several ways to obtain on-line Help. These are:

On-line Help Messages: Word displays a command description in the Status bar when you choose a menu or command.

Context Sensitive Help: Simply press **F1** to get instant help on any menu function or formatting action that you are carrying out. If you are not using a menu box you will bring up the Answer Wizard. Pressing <Esc>, or clicking the **Cancel** button, will close the Answer Wizard and return you to your original screen.

Another way of getting context sensitive help is to click the Help button on the Toolbar, shown here, then move the modified mouse pointer to an area of the document or onto a particular Toolbar button and press the left mouse button.

Further help can be obtained by selecting **Help**, then the **Microsoft Word Help Topics** and pressing the Index tab. Typing the first few letters of the word you are looking for, causes the program to jump to the nearest word, as follows:

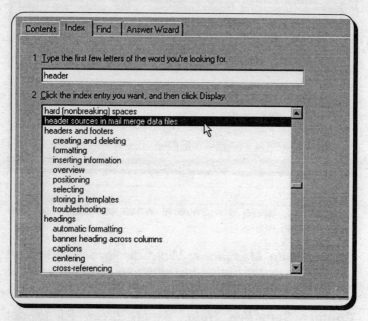

If you were to select *headers and footers*, then press the **Display** button, a further list would appear. Selecting *Add page numbers* from this list and pressing **Display**, produces a further window with more specific information. Many Help topics contain cross-references

to other related Help topics. When the mouse pointer rests on such cross-references, it changes to a pointing hand. These are often known as 'hypertext' links, and clicking the hand pointer on them displays further information.

The Find tab on the **Microsoft Word Help Topics** window works in the same way as the Index tab.

3. WORD DOCUMENT BASICS

When the program is first used, all Word's features default to those shown on page 14. It is quite possible to use Word in this mode, without changing any main settings, but obviously it is possible to customise the package to your exact needs, as we shall see later.

Entering Text

In order to illustrate some of Word's capabilities, you need to have a short text at hand. We suggest you type the memo displayed below into a new document. At this stage, don't worry if the length of the lines below differ from those on your display.

As you type in text, any time you want to force a new line, or paragraph, just press <Enter>. While typing within a paragraph, Word sorts out line lengths automatically (known as 'word wrap'), without you having to press any keys to move to a new line. If you make a mistake while typing, press the <BkSp> key enough times to erase the mistake and start again.

MEMO TO PC USERS

Networked Computers

The microcomputers in the Data Processing room are a mixture of IBM compatible PCs with either 486 or Pentium processors. They all have 3.5" floppy drives of 1.44MB capacity, and some also have CD-ROM drives. The PCs are connected to various printers via a network; the Laser printers available giving best output.

The computer you are using will have at least a 540MB capacity hard disc on which a number of software programs, including the latest version of Windows, have been installed. To make life easier, the hard disc is highly structured with each program installed in a separate folder (directory).

Moving Around a Document

You can move the cursor around a document with the normal direction keys, and with the key combinations listed below.

To move	Press
Left one character	←
Right one character	→
Up one line	↑
Down one line	↓
Left one word	Ctrl+←
Right one word	Ctrl+→
To beginning of line	Home
To end of line	End
To paragraph beginning	Ctrl+↑
To paragraph end	Ctrl+↓
Up one screen	PgUp
Down one screen	PgDn
To top of previous page	Ctrl+PgUp
To top of next page	Ctrl+PgDn
To beginning of file	Ctrl+Home
To end of file	Ctrl+End

In a multi-page document, use the **Edit**, **Go To** command (or <Ctrl+G>), to jump to a specified page number.

Obviously, you need to become familiar with the above methods of moving the cursor around a document, particularly if you are not using a mouse and you spot an error in a document which needs to be corrected, which is the subject of the next chapter.

Templates and Paragraph Styles

When you start Word for the first time, the Style Status box (at the extreme left of the Formatting bar) contains the word **Normal**. This means that all the text you have entered, at the moment, is shown in the Normal paragraph style which is one of the styles available in the NORMAL template. Every document produced by Word has to use a template, and NORMAL is the default. A template contains, both the document page settings and a set of formatting instructions which can be applied to text.

Changing Paragraph Styles:

To change the style of a paragraph, do the following:

- Place the cursor (insertion pointer) on the paragraph in question, say the title line

- Left click the Style Status button, and select the **Heading 1** style.

The selected paragraph reformats instantly in bold, and in Arial typeface of point size 14.

With the cursor in the second line of text, select **Heading 3** which reformats the line in Arial 12. Your memo should now look presentable, as shown below.

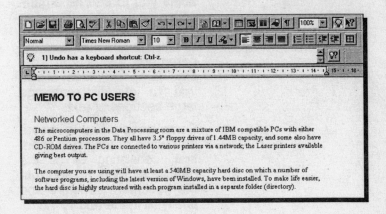

Document Screen Displays

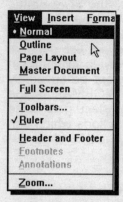

Word provides four display modes, Normal, Outline, Page Layout, and Master Document, as well as the options to view your documents in a whole range of screen enlargements by selecting **Zoom**. You control all these viewing options with the **View** sub-menu, shown here, and when a document is displayed you can switch freely between them. When first loaded the screen displays in Normal mode.

The mode options have the following effect, and some can also be accessed by clicking the View buttons on the left of the Status bar.

Normal

Returns you to normal viewing from either Outline or Page Layout viewing mode.

Outline

Provides a collapsible view of a document, which enables you to see its organisation at a glance. You can display all the text in a file, or just the text that uses the paragraph styles you specify. Using this mode, allows you to quickly rearrange large sections of text.

Some people like to create an outline of their document first, consisting of all the headings, then to sort out the document structure and finally fill in the text.

Page Layout

Provides a WYSIWYG (what you see is what you get) view of a document. The text displays in the typefaces and point sizes you specify, and with the selected attributes (alignment, indention, spacing, etc.). All frames, tables, graphics, headers, footers, and footnotes appear on the screen as they will in the final printed document.

Master Document

Provides you with an outline view of a document that takes its contents from one or more Word documents. For example, each chapter of a book could be made into a sub-document of such a Master Document. The Master Document could then be used to reorganise, add or remove sub-documents. Selecting this mode, causes Word to display the Master Document and Outline toolbars.

Full Screen

Presents you with a clean, uncluttered screen; the Toolbars, Ruler, Scroll bars, and Status bar are removed. To return to the usual screen, click the 'Full' icon, shown here, which appears at the bottom of your screen when in this mode.

Zoom   Allows you to change the
viewing magnification factor
from its default value of
100%. This can
also be changed
by clicking the
'Zoom Control'
icon on the Tool-
bar. Clicking its
down   arrow
button,   reveals
other magnifica-
tion factors, as shown here.

Changing Default Options

Modifying Margins:

To change the standard page margins for your entire
document from the cursor position onward, or for
selected text (more about this later), do the following:

* Select the **File, Page Set**u**p** command

* Click the left mouse button at the **Margins** tab
  on the displayed dialogue box, shown below.

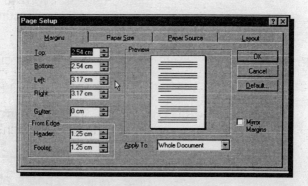

The 'Preview' page in the middle of the box shows how
your changes will look on a real page.

Changing the Default Paper Size:

To change the default paper size from the size set
during installation to a different size, do the following:

- Select the **File, Page Setup** command

- Click the left mouse button at the **Paper Size** tab
  on the displayed dialogue box, shown below

- Click the down-arrow against the **Paper Size**
  box to reveal the list of available paper sizes

- Change the page size to your new choice, and
  press the **Default** button and confirm that you
  wish this change to affect all new documents
  based on the NORMAL template.

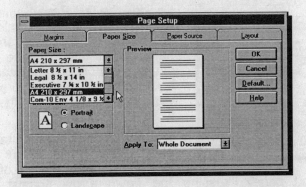

Check that the paper size matches that in your printer,
otherwise you may get strange results. The orientation
of the printed page is normally **Portrait** (text prints
across the page width), but you could choose to
change this to **Landscape** which prints across the
page length, as long as your printer can print in
landscape.

Modifying the Paper Source:

Clicking on the third Page Setup tab, displays yet

another dialogue box, part of which is shown here, from which you can select the paper source. You might have a printer that holds paper in trays, in which case you might want to specify that the first page (headed paper perhaps), should be taken from one tray, while the rest of the paper should be taken from a different tray.

Modifying the Page Layout:

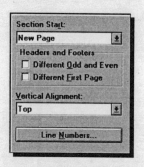

Clicking the last Page Setup tab displays the Layout dialogue box, part of which is shown here. From this dialogue box you can set options for headers and footers, section breaks, vertical alignment and whether to add line numbers.

The default for **Section Start** is 'New Page' which allows the section to start at the top of the next page. Pressing the down arrow against this option, allows you to change this choice.

In the Headers and Footers box you can specify whether you want one header or footer for even-numbered pages and a different header or footer for odd-numbered pages. You can further specify if you want a different header or footer on the first page from the header or footer used for the rest of the document. Word can align the top line with the 'Top' margin, but this can be changed with the **Vertical Alignment** option.

Changing Other Default Options:

You can also change the default options available to you in Word for Windows, by selecting the **Tools, Options** command. Using the displayed Options dialogue box (shown below) you can:

- Specify the default **View** options. For example, you can select whether non-printing characters, such as Tabs, Spaces, and Paragraph marks, are shown or not.

- Adjust the **General** Word settings, such as the colour of text and its background, and the units of measure.

- Adjust the **Print** settings, such as the **Reverse Print Order** mode, or choose to print the **Summary** Info or **Annotations**.

- Change the **Save** options, such as selecting the **Always Create Backup Copy** option for your work.

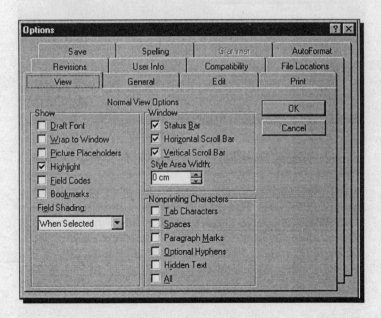

Saving to a File

To save a document to disc, use either of the following two commands:

- **File, Save** which is used when a document has previously been saved to disc in a named file; using this command automatically saves your work under the existing filename without prompting you.

- **File, Save As** command which is used when you want to save your document with a different name from the one you gave it already.

Using the **File, Save As** command (or the very first time you use the **File, Save** command when a document has no name), causes the following dialogue box to appear on your screen:

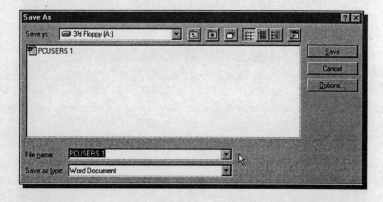

Note that the old document name (if it exists) is highlighted in the **File name** field box and the program is waiting for you to type a new name. Any name you type (don't use more than 255 characters) will replace the existing name. Filenames cannot include any of the following keyboard characters: /, \, >, <, *, ?, ", |, :, or ;. Word adds the file extension **.DOC** automatically and uses it to identify the document, but you don't see it.

You can select a drive other than the one displayed, by clicking the down arrow against the **Save in** field. To save your work currently in memory, move the cursor into the **File name** box, and type **PCUSERS 1**.

By clicking the **Save as type** button at the bottom of the Save As dialogue box, you can save the Document Template, or the Text Only parts of your work, or you can save your document in a variety of other formats, such as MS-DOS Text, Rich Text Format, or a number of WordPerfect formats.

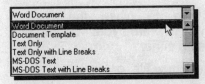

Document Properties:

A useful feature in Word is the facility to add document properties to every file by selecting the **File, Properties** command. A Properties box, as shown below, opens for you to type additional information about your document.

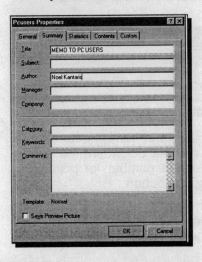

In this box you can select to add a manager, company, or category name to group files together for ease of retrieval.

To do this on a more regular basis, make sure that the **Prompt for Document Properties** box in the Save Options dialogue box is selected and appears ticked.

Closing a Document:

There are several ways to close a document in Word. Once you have saved it you can click its 'x' close button, or double-click on the Document Control button at the left end of the menu bar; you would usually use these when you have several files open together.

If you want to close the current document, then open a new or another document, do the following:

- Choose **File, Close** to close the current document (remove it from your computer's memory) before using either

- **File, New** to create a new file, or

- **File, Open** to use an existing file.

If the document (or file) has changed since the last time it was saved, you will be given the option to save it before it is removed from memory.

If a document is not closed before a new document is opened, then both documents will be held in memory, but only one will be the current document. To find out which documents are held in memory, use the **Window** command to reveal the following menu:

In this case, the first document in the list is the current document, and to make another document the current one, either type the document number, or point at its name and click the left mouse button.

To close a document which is not the current document, use the **Window** command, make it current, and close it with one of the above methods.

34

4. EDITING WORD DOCUMENTS

It will not be long, when using Word, before you will need to edit your document. One of the first things you will notice is that misspelled words are unobtrusively underlined in a red wavy line, as shown here, and that the Tip Wizard advises you to right-click these words to correct them. This is possibly the most time-saving enhancement in the spell checker (to be discussed later).

Computors

Other editing could include deleting unwanted words or adding extra text in the document. All these operations are very easy to carry out.

For small deletions, such as letters or words, the easiest method to adopt is the use of the <Del> or <BkSp> keys. With the <Del> key, position the cursor on the left of the first letter you want to delete and press <Del>; the letter is deleted and the following text moves one space to the left. With the <BkSp> key, position the cursor immediately to the right of the character to be deleted and press <BkSp>; the cursor moves one space to the left pulling the rest of the line with it and overwriting the character to be deleted.

Word processing is usually carried out in the insert mode. Any characters typed will be inserted at the cursor location (insertion point) and the following text will be pushed to the right, and down, to make room. To insert blank lines in your text, place the cursor at the beginning of the line where the blank line is needed and press <Enter>. To remove the blank line, position the cursor on it and press <Del>.

When larger scale editing is needed you have several alternatives. You could first 'select' the text to be altered, then use the **Cut, Copy** and **Paste** operations available in the **Edit** sub-menu, or click on Toolbar button alternatives. Another method is to use the 'drag and drop' facility for copying or moving text.

Selecting Text

The procedure in Word, as with most Windows based applications, is first to select the text to be altered before any operation, such as formatting or editing, can be carried out on it. Selected text is highlighted on the screen. This can be carried out in two main ways:

A. Using the keyboard, to select:

- A block of text.

  Position the cursor on the first character to be selected and hold down the <Shift> key while using the arrow keys to highlight the required text, then release the <Shift> key.

- A word.

  Use <Shift+End>.

- From the present cursor position to the beginning of the line.

  Use <Shift+Home>.

- From the present cursor position to the end of the document.

  Use <Shift+Ctrl+End>.

- From the present cursor position to the beginning of the document.

  Use <Shift+Ctrl+Home>.

B. With the mouse, to select:

- A block of text.

  Press down the left mouse button at the beginning of the block and while holding it pressed, drag the cursor across the block so that the desired text is highlighted, then release the mouse button.

- A word.

  Double-click within the word.

- A line.

  Place the mouse pointer on the selection bar, just to the left of the line, and click once (for multiple lines, after selecting the first line, drag the pointer in the selection bar).

- A sentence.

  Hold the <Ctrl> key down and click in the sentence.

- A paragraph.

  Place the mouse pointer in the selection bar and double-click (for multiple paragraphs, after selecting the first paragraph, drag the pointer in the selection bar).

- The whole document.

  Place the mouse pointer in the selection bar, hold the <Ctrl> key down and click once.

Copying Blocks of Text

Once text has been selected it can be copied to another location in your present document, to another Word document, or to another Windows application, via the clipboard. As with most of the editing and formatting operations there are several alternative ways of doing this, as follows:

*   Use the **Edit, Copy** command sequence from the menu, to copy the selected text to the Windows clipboard, moving the cursor to the start of where you want the copied text to be placed, and using the **Edit, Paste** command.

*   Use the quick key combinations, <Ctrl+Ins> (or <Ctrl+C>) to copy and <Shift+Ins> (or <Ctrl+V>) to paste, once the text to be copied has been selected, which does not require the menu bar to be activated.

*   Use the 'Copy to clipboard' and 'Paste from clipboard' Toolbar buttons; you can of course only use this method with a mouse.

To copy the same text again to another location, to any open window document or application, move the cursor to the new location and paste it there with any of these methods, as it is stored on the clipboard until it is replaced by the next Cut, or Copy operation.

*   First select the text, then hold both the <Ctrl> and <Shift> keys depressed, place the cursor at the start of where you want the copied text to be and press the right mouse button. The new text will insert itself where placed, even if the overstrike mode is in operation. Text copied by this method is not placed on the clipboard, so multiple copies are not possible, as with the other methods.

Moving Blocks of Text

Selected text can be moved to any location in the same document by either of the following:

- Using the **Edit, Cut,** command or <Shift+Del> (or <Ctrl+X>).

- Clicking the 'Cut to clipboard' Toolbar button, shown here.

Next, move the cursor to the required new location and use either of the following procedures:

- The **Edit, Paste** command.

- Any other paste actions as described previously.

The moved text will be placed at the cursor location and will force any existing text to make room for it. This operation can be cancelled by simply pressing <Esc>. Once moved, multiple copies of the same text can be produced by other **Paste** operations.

Selected text can be moved by dragging the mouse with the left button held down. The drag pointer is an arrow with an attached square - the vertical dotted line showing the point of insertion.

Deleting Blocks of Text

When text is 'cut' it is removed from the document, but placed on the clipboard until further text is either copied or cut. With Word any selected text can be deleted by pressing **Edit, Cut,** or by pressing the <Del>, or <BkSp> keys. However, using **Edit, Cut,** allows you to use the **Edit, Paste** command, but using the <Del> or <BkSp> keys, does not.

The Undo Command

As text is lost with the delete command, you should use it with caution, but if you do make a mistake all is not lost as long as you act promptly. The **Edit, Undo** command or <Ctrl+Z> (or <Alt+BkSp>) reverses your most recent editing or formatting commands.

You can also use the Toolbar buttons, shown here, to

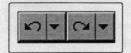 undo one of several editing or formatting mistakes (press the down arrow to the right of the left button to see a list of your changes) or even redo any one of the undo moves with the right button.

Undo does not reverse any action once editing changes have been saved to file. Only editing done since the last save can be reversed.

Finding and Changing Text

Word allows you to search for specifically selected text, or character combinations. To do this use:

• The **Find** or the **Replace** option from the **Edit** command sub-menu.

Using the **Find** option (<Ctrl+F>), will highlight each occurrence of the supplied text in turn so that you can carry out some action on it, such as change its font or appearance.

Using the **Replace** option (<Ctrl+H>), allows you to specify what replacement is to be automatically carried out. For example, in a long article you may decide to replace every occurrence of the word 'microcomputers' with the word 'PCs'.

40

To illustrate the **Replace** procedure, either select the option from the **Edit** sub-menu or use the quick key combination <Ctrl+H>. This opens the Replace dialogue box, displayed in the top half of the composite screen dump shown below.

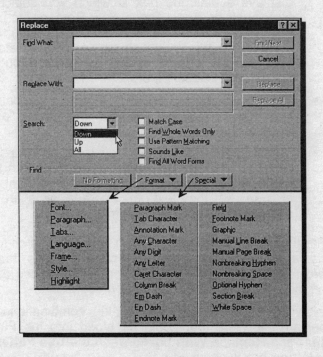

Towards the bottom of the dialogue box, there are five check boxes; the first two can be used to match the case of letters in the search string, and/or a whole word, while the last three can be used for pattern, 'sounds like' or 'word forms' matching.

The two buttons, **Format** and **Special**, situated at the bottom of the dialogue box, let you control how the search is carried out. The lists of available options, when either of these buttons is pressed, are displayed above. You will of course only see one or the other, but not both as shown here.

You can force both the search and the replace operations to work with exact text attributes. For example, selecting:

- The **Font** option from the list under **Format**, displays a dialogue box in which you select a font (such as Arial, Times New Roman, etc.); a font-style (such as regular, bold, italic, etc.); an underline option (such as single, double, etc.); and special effects (such as strike-through, superscript, subscript, etc.).

- The **Paragraph** option, lets you control indentation, spacing (before and after), and alignment.

- The **Style** option, allows you to search for, or replace, different paragraph styles. This can be useful if you develop a new style and want to change all the text of another style in a document to use your preferred style.

With the use of the **Special** button, you can search for, and replace, various specified document marks, tabs, hard returns, etc., or a combination of both these and text, as listed in the previous screen dump.

Below we list only two of the many key combinations of special characters that could be typed into the **Find What** and **Replace With** boxes when the **Use Pattern Matching** box is checked.

Type	*To find or replace*
?	Any single character within a pattern. For example, searching for nec?, will find <u>neck</u>, con<u>nect</u>, etc.
*	Any string of characters. For example, searching for c*r, will find such words as <u>cellar</u>, <u>chillier</u>, etc., also parts of words such as <u>character</u>, and combinations of words such as <u>connect, cellar</u>

Page Breaks

The program automatically inserts a 'soft' page break in a document when a page of typed text is full. To force a manual, or hard page break, either type <Ctrl+Enter> or use the **Insert**, **Break** command and select **Page Break** in the dialogue box, as shown below.

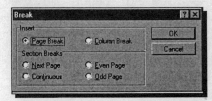

Pressing **OK** places a series of dots across the page to indicate the page break, as shown below. To delete manual page breaks place the cursor on the selection bar to the left of the page break mark, click once to highlight the line of dots, and press <Del>.

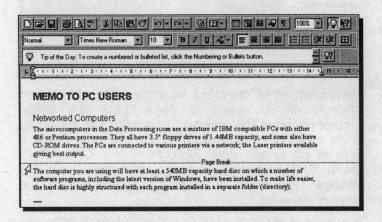

Soft page breaks which are automatically entered by the program at the end of pages, cannot be deleted.

Using the Spell Checker

The package has a very comprehensive spell checker which whenever it thinks it has found a misspelled word, underlines it with a red wavy line. To correct your document, right-click such words for alternatives.

However, the spell checker can also be used in another way. To spell check your document, either click the 'Spelling' button on the Standard Toolbar, shown here, or use the **Tools**, **Spelling** command (or **F7**) to open the dialogue box shown below (if necessary, use the **Tools, Language** command, select the correct dictionary and click the **Default** button).

Word starts spell checking from the point of insertion onwards. If you want to spell check the whole document, move the insertion pointer to the beginning of the document before starting. If you want to check a word or paragraph only, highlight it first. Once Word has found a misspelled word, you can correct it in the **Change To** box, or select a word from the **Suggestions** list.

The main dictionary cannot be edited. However, the system has the ability to add specialised and personal dictionaries with the facility to customise and edit the latter. If you are using personal dictionaries and you use the spell checker and choose **Add**, the specified word is added to the dictionary.

Printing Documents

When Windows was first installed on your computer the printers you intend to use should have been selected, and the SETUP program should have installed the appropriate printer drivers. Before printing for the first time, you would be wise to ensure that your printer is in fact properly installed. To do this, click on **Start** then select **Settings** and click the **Printers** menu option to open the Printers dialogue box shown below.

Here, two printer drivers have been installed; an HP LaserJet 4M as the 'default' printer and an HP LaserJet 4/4M PostScript. In our case these are both configured to output to a printer via the parallel port LPT1. This refers to the socket at the back of your PC which is connected to your printer. LPT1 is short for Line Printer No. 1. Your selections may, obviously, not be the same.

To see how a printer is configured (whether to print to the parallel port or to a file), select it by clicking its icon, use the **File, Properties** command and click the Details tab of the displayed dialogue box.

Next, return to or reactivate Word and, if the document you want to print is not in memory, either click the 'Open' button on the Toolbar, or use the **File, Open** command, to display the Open dialogue box shown overleaf.

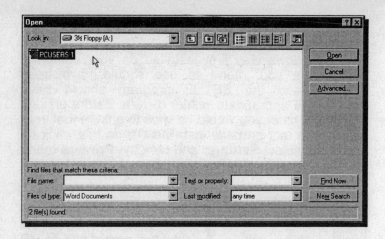

Use this dialogue box to locate the file (document) you want to print, which will be found on the drive and folder (directory) on which you saved it originally. Select it and click the **Open** button (or double-click its name), to load it into your computer's memory.

To print your document, do one of the following:

- Click the Print icon on the Toolbar, shown here, which prints the document using the current defaults.

- Use the **File, Print** command which opens the 'Print' box, shown below.

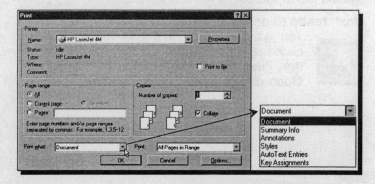

The settings in the Print dialogue box allow you to select the number of copies, and which pages, you want printed. You can also select to print the document, the summary information relating to that document, annotations, styles, etc., as shown in the drop-down list also on the previous page.

You can even change the selected printer by clicking the down arrow against the **Printer Name** box which displays the available printers on your system.

Clicking the **Properties** button on the Print dialogue box, displays the Properties dialogue box for the selected printer, shown below, which allows you to select the paper size, orientation needed, paper source, etc.

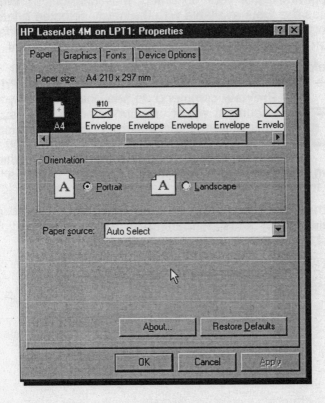

The **Options** button on the Print dialogue box, gives you access to some more advanced print options, such as printing in reverse order, with or without annotations, print hidden text or field codes, etc.

Clicking the **OK** button on these various multi-level dialogue boxes, causes Word to accept your selections and return you to the previous level dialogue box, until the Print dialogue box is reached. Selecting **OK** on this first level dialogue box, sends print output from Word to your selection, either the printer connected to your computer, or to an encoded file on disc. Selecting **Cancel** or **Close** on any level dialogue box, aborts the selections made at that level.

Do remember that, whenever you change printers, the appearance of your document may change, as Word uses the fonts available with the newly selected printer. This can affect the line lengths, which in turn will affect both the tabulation and pagination of your document.

Before printing to paper, click the Print Preview icon on the Toolbar, shown here, or use the **File, Print** **Preview** command, to see how much of your document will fit on your selected page size. This depends very much on the chosen font. Thus, the **Print Preview** option allows you to see the layout of the final printed page, which can save a few trees and equally important to you, a lot of frustration and wear and tear on your printer.

Other enhancements of your document, such as selection of fonts, formatting of text, and pagination, will be discussed in the next chapter.

5. FORMATTING WORD DOCUMENTS

Formatting involves the appearance of individual words or even characters, the line spacing and alignment of paragraphs, and the overall page layout of the entire document. These functions are carried out in Word in several different ways.

Primary page layout is included in a document's Template and text formatting in a Template's styles. Within any document, however, you can override Paragraph Style formats by applying text formatting and enhancements manually to selected text. To immediately cancel manual formatting, select the text and use the

Edit, Undo

command, or (<Ctrl+Z>). The selected text reverts to its original format.

In the long term, you can cancel manual formatting by selecting the text and using the <Shift+Ctrl+N> key stroke. The text then reverts to its style format.

Formatting Text

If you use TrueType fonts, which are automatically installed when you set up Windows, Word uses the same font to display text on the screen and to print on paper. The screen fonts provide a very close approximation of printed characters. TrueType font names are preceded by 🐝 in the Font box on the Formatting toolbar and in the Font dialog box which displays when you use the **Format, Font** command.

If you use non-TrueType fonts, then use a screen font that matches your printer font. If a matching font is not available, or if your printer driver does not provide screen font information, Windows chooses the screen font that most closely resembles the printer font.

Originally, the title of the memo **PCUSERS 1**, was typed in the 14 point size Arial typeface, while the subtitle and the main text were typed in 12 and 10 point size Arial, respectively.

To change this memo into what appears on the screen dump displayed below, first select the title of the memo and format it to bold, italics, 18 point size Arial and centre it between the margins, then select the subtitle and format it to bold, 14 point size Arial.

Finally select each paragraph of the main body of the memo in turn, and format it to 12 point size Times New Roman. All of this formatting can be achieved by using the buttons on the Formatting bar shown below (see also the section entitled 'Paragraph Alignment').

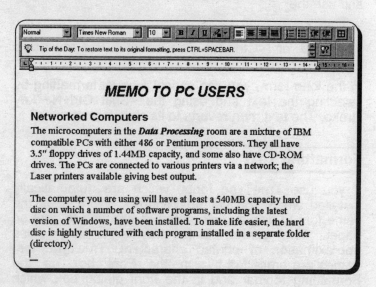

If you can't access these font styles, it will probably be because your printer does not support them, in which case you will need to select other fonts that are supported.

Save the result under the new filename **PCUSERS 2** - use the **File, Save As** command.

In Word all manual formatting, including the selection of font, point size, style (bold, italic, highlight, strikethrough, hidden and capitals), colour, super/subscript, and various underlines, are carried out by first selecting the text and then executing the formatting command.

The easiest way of activating the formatting commands is from the Formatting toolbar. Another way is to use the

Format, Font

command, which displays the following dialogue box:

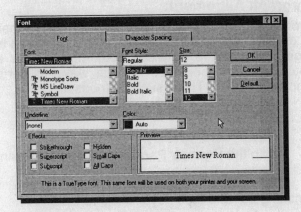

Yet another method is by using quick keys, some of which are listed below:

To Format	*Type*
Bold	Ctrl+B
Italic	Ctrl+I
Underline	Ctrl+U
Word underline	Ctrl+Shift+W
Double underline	Ctrl+Shift+D

There are quick keys to do almost anything, but the problem is remembering them! We find that those listed here are the most useful and the easiest to remember.

Text Enhancements

Word defines a paragraph, as any text which is followed by a paragraph mark, which is created by pressing the <Enter> key. So single line titles, as well as long typed text, can form paragraphs.

 The paragraph symbol, shown here, is only visible if you have selected it from the Toolbar.

Paragraph Alignment:

Word allows you to align a paragraph at the left margin (the default), at the right margin, centred between both margins, or justified between both margins. As with most operations there are several ways to perform alignment in Word. Three such methods are:

- Using buttons on the **Formatting bar**.
- Using keyboard short cuts, when available.
- Using the **Format**, **Paragraph** menu command.

The table below describes the buttons on the Formatting bar and their keystroke shortcuts.

Buttons on Formatting bar	Paragraph Alignment	Keystrokes
	Left	<Ctrl+L>
	Centred	<Ctrl+E>
	Right	<Ctrl+R>
	Justified	<Ctrl+J>

The display below shows the dialogue box resulting from using the **Format**, **Paragraph** command in which you can specify any **Left, Right**, or **Special** indentation required.

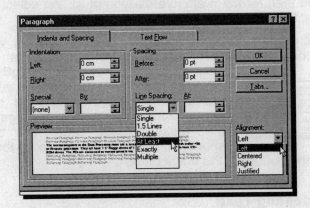

Paragraph Spacing:

The above Paragraph dialogue box can also be used to display a paragraph on screen, or print it on paper, in single-line, 1½-line, or double-line spacing. You can even set the spacing to any value you want by using the **At Least** option, as shown on the above screen dump, then specify what interval you want.

The available shortcut keys for paragraph spacing are as follows:

To Format	*Type*
Single-spaced lines	Ctrl+1
One-and-a-half-spaced lines	Ctrl+5
Double-spaced lines	Ctrl+2

Whichever of the above methods is used, formatting can take place either before or after the text is entered. If formatting is selected first, then text will type in the chosen format until a further formatting command is given. If, on the other hand, you choose to enter text and then format it afterwards, you must first select the text to be formatted, then activate the formatting.

Word gives you the choice of 4 units to work with, inches, centimetres, points or picas. These can be selected by using the **Tools**, **Options** command, choosing the **General** tab of the displayed Options dialogue box, and clicking the down arrow against the **Measurement Units** list box, shown open here, which is to be found at the bottom of the dialogue box.

Indenting Text:

Most documents will require some form of paragraph indenting. An indent is the space between the margin and the edge of the text in the paragraph. When an indent is set (on the left or right side of the page), any justification on that side of the page sets at the indent, not the page border.

To illustrate indentation, open the file **PCUSERS 2**, select the first paragraph, and then choose the **Format**, **Paragraph** command. In the **Indentation** field, select 2.5cm for both **Left** and **Right**, as shown on the next page. On clicking **OK**, the first selected paragraph is displayed indented. Our screen dump shows the result of the indentation as well as the settings on the Paragraph dialogue box which caused it.

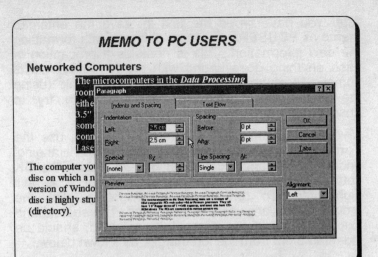

MEMO TO PC USERS

Networked Computers

The microcomputers in the *Data Processing*
room
eith
3.5"
som
conn
Lase

The computer you
disc on which a n
version of Windo
disc is highly stru
(directory).

The **Indentation** option in the Paragraph dialogue box, can be used to create 'hanging' indents, where all the lines in a paragraph, including any text on the first line that follows a tab, are indented by a specified amount. This is often used in lists to emphasise certain points.

To illustrate the method, use the **PCUSERS 1** file and add at the end of it the text shown below.

In Windows 95 you can work with files in three different ways:

Name Description

My Computer Use the My Computer utility which Microsoft have spent much time and effort making as intuitive as possible.

Explorer Use the Windows Explorer, a much improved version of the older File Manager.

MS-DOS Use an MS-DOS Prompt window if you prefer to and are an expert with the DOS commands.

After you have typed the text in, save the enlarged memo as **PCUSERS 3**, before going on with formatting the new information. This is done as a precaution in case anything goes wrong with the formatting - it is sometimes much easier to reload a saved file (using the **File, Open** command), than it is to try to unscramble a wrongly formatted document!

Next, highlight the last 4 paragraphs above, use the **Format**, **Paragraph** command, and select 'Hanging' under **Special** and 3 cm under **By**. On clicking the **OK** button, the text formats as shown, but it is still highlighted. To remove the highlighting, click the mouse button anywhere on the page. The second and following lines of the paragraphs selected, should be indented 3 cm from the left margin, as shown below.

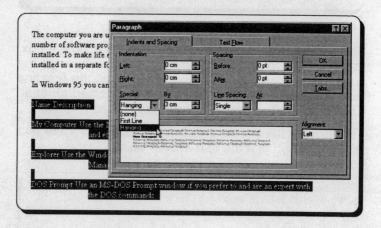

This is still not very inspiring, so to complete the effect we will edit the first lines of each paragraph as follows:

Place the cursor in front of the word 'Description' and press the <Tab> key once. This places the start of the word in the same column as the indented text of the other paragraphs. To complete the effect place tabs before the words 'Use' in the next three paragraphs, until your hanging indents are correct, as shown on the next page.

In Windows 95 you can work with files in three different ways:

Name	Description
My Computer	Use the My Computer utility which Microsoft have spent much time and effort making as intuitive as possible.
Explorer	Use the Windows Explorer, a much improved version of the older File Manager.
MS-DOS	Use an MS-DOS Prompt window if you prefer to and are an expert with the DOS commands.

This may seem like a complicated rigmarole to go through each time you want the hanging indent effect, but with Word you will eventually set up all your indents, etc., as styles in templates. Then all you do is click in a paragraph to produce them.

When you finish formatting the document, save it under its current filename either with the **File, Save** command (<Ctrl+S>), or by clicking the Save button. This command does not display a dialogue box, so you use it when you do not need to make any changes to the saving operation.

Inserting Bullets:

Bullets are small characters you can insert, anywhere you like, in the text of your document to improve visual impact. In Word there are several choices for displaying lists with bullets or numbers. As well as the two Formatting bar buttons, others are made available through the

F_ormat, Bullets and N_umbering

command, which displays the following dialogue box:

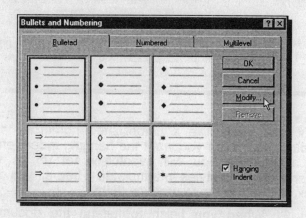

You can select any of the bullets shown here, or you could click the **Modify** button to change the size of the bullet, or the indentation.

Further, by pressing the **Bullet** button on the Modify Bulleted List dialogue box which would be displayed, you could select any character from the Symbol typeface or other available type-faces.

If you select the **Numbered** or **Multilevel** tab, a similar dialogue box is displayed, giving you a choice of several numbering or multilevel systems.

Once inserted, you can copy, move or cut a bulleted line in the same way as any other text. However, you can not delete a bullet with the <BkSp> or <Del> keys.

Formatting with Page Tabs

You can format text in columns by using tab stops.
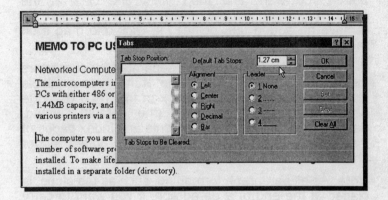 Word has default left tab stops every 1.27 cm
from the left margin, as shown here. This symbol
appears on the left edge of the ruler (see below).

To set tabs, use either the **Format**, **Tabs** command
which produces the Tab dialogue box, or click on the
tab symbol on the left of the Ruler which cycles
through the available tab stops.

The tab stop types available have the following
function:

Button	*Name*	*Effect*
	Left	Left aligns text after the tab stop.
	Centre	Centres text on tab stop.
	Right	Right aligns text after the tab stop.
	Decimal	Aligns decimal point with tab stop.

59

To clear the ruler of tab settings press the **Clear All** button in the Tabs dialogue box. When you set a tab stop on the ruler, all default tab stops to the left of the one you are setting are removed. In addition, tab stops apply either to the paragraph containing the cursor, or to any selected paragraphs.

The easiest way to set a tab is to click on the tab type button you want and then point and click at the required position on the lower half of the ruler. To remove an added tab, point to it, click and drag it off the ruler.

If you want tabular text to be separated by characters instead of by spaces, select one of the three available characters from the **Leader** box in the Tabs dialogue box. The options are none (the default), dotted, dashed, or underline. The Contents and Index pages of this book are set with right tabs and dotted leader characters.

Note: As all paragraph formatting, such as tab stops, is placed at the end of a paragraph, if you want to carry the formatting of the current paragraph to the next, press <Enter>. If you don't want formatting to carry on, press the down arrow key instead.

Formatting with Styles

We saw earlier in Chapter 5, how you can format your work using Paragraph Styles, but we confined ourselves to using the default **Normal** style only. In this section we will get to grips with how to create, modify, use, and manage styles.

As mentioned previously, a Paragraph Style is a set of formatting instructions which you save so that you can use repeatedly within a document or in different documents. A collection of Paragraph Styles can be placed in a Template which could be appropriate for, say, all your memos, so it can be used to preserve uniformity. It maintains consistency and saves time by not having to format each paragraph individually.

Further, should you decide to change a style, all the paragraphs associated with that style reformat automatically. Finally, if you want to provide a pattern for shaping a final document, then you use what is known as a Template. All documents which have not been assigned a document template, use the **Normal.dot** global template, by default.

Paragraph Styles:

Paragraph Styles contain paragraph and character formats and a name can be attached to these formatting instructions. From then on, applying the style name is the same as formatting that paragraph with the same instructions.

You can create a style by example, either with the use of the Formatting bar or the keyboard, or you can create a style from scratch, before you use it, by selecting the **Format, Style** menu command. By far the simplest way of creating a style is by example.

Creating Paragraph Styles by Example: Previously, we spent some time manually creating some hanging indents in the last few paragraphs of the **PCUSERS 3** document. To create a style from this previous work, place the insertion pointer in one of these paragraphs, say, in the 'Name Description' line, and highlight the entire name of the existing style in the Formatting bar's Style box, as shown below.

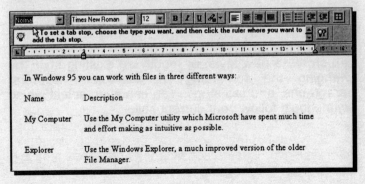

Then, type the new style name you want to create, say, 'Hanging Indent', and press <Enter>.

Finally, highlight the last three paragraphs with hanging indents and change their style to the new 'Hanging Indent', by clicking the mouse in the Style box button and selecting the appropriate style from the displayed list, as shown below. Save the result as **PCUSERS 4.**

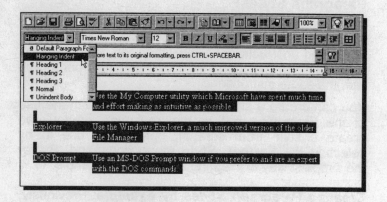

Creating Styles with the Menu Command: You can create, or change, a style before you apply any formatting to a paragraph, by using the **Format**, **Style** command. This displays the Style dialogue box, in which you can choose which style you want to change from the displayed **Styles** list.

Having selected the style you want to change (or not, as the case may be), click the **Modify** button which produces the Modify Style dialogue box. From here you can create a new style, or modify an existing style, by changing the formatting of characters, borders, paragraphs, and tab stops. You can even select which style should follow your current style.

Document Templates

A document template provides the overall pattern of your final document. It can contain:

- Styles to control your paragraph and formats.

- Page set-up options.

- Boilerplate text, which is text that remains the same in every document.

- AutoText (Glossary in previous versions), which is standard text and graphics that you could insert in a document by typing the name of the AutoText entry.

- Macros, which are programs that can change the menus and key assignments to comply with the type of document you are creating.

- Customised shortcuts, toolbars and menus.

If you don't assign a template to a document, then the default **Normal.dot** template is used by Word. To create a new document template, you either modify an existing one, create one from scratch, or create one based on the formatting of an existing document.

Creating a Document Template:

To illustrate the last point above, we will create a simple document template, which we will call **PCuser**, based on the formatting of the **PCUSERS 4** document. But first, make sure you have defined the 'Hanging Indent' style as explained earlier.

To create a template based on an existing document:

- Open the existing document.

- Select the **File, Save As** command which displays the Save As dialogue box, shown overleaf.

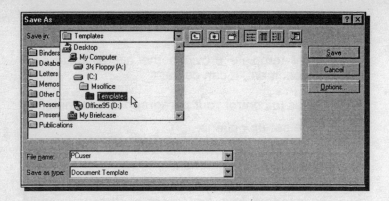

- In the **Save as type** box, select Document Template.

- In the **Save in** box, use the Templates folder which is in the Msoffice folder, which should have opened for you.

- In the **File name** box, type the name of the new template (PCuser in our example).

- Press the **Save** button, which opens the template file **PCuser.dot** in the Word working area.

- Add the text and graphics you want to appear in all new documents that you base on this template, and *delete* any items (including text) you do not want to appear (In our example, we deleted everything in the document, bar the heading).

- Click the Save icon on the Toolbar, and close the document.

To use the new template, do the following:

- Use the **File**, **New** command which causes the New dialogue box to be displayed, as shown on the next page.

64

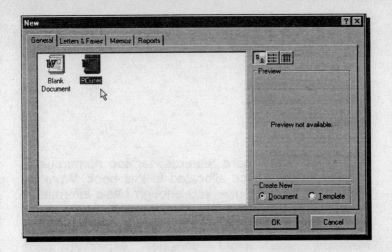

- Click the General tab and select the name of the template you want to use from the displayed list.

- Make sure that the radio button **Document** is selected, and click the **OK** button.

The new document will be using the selected template.

Templates can also contain Macros as well as AutoText; macros allow you to automate Word keystroke actions only, while AutoText speeds up the addition of boilerplate text and graphics into your document. However, the design of these features is beyond the scope of this book.

On the other hand, Word has a series of built-in templates to suit every occasion. These can be found, as seen in the above dialogue box, under the tabs of Letters & Faxes, Memos, and Reports. Try them.

* * *

Word has many more features, far too numerous to mention in the space allocated to this book. What we have tried to do is give you enough basic information so that you can have the confidence to forge ahead and explore the rest of its capabilities by yourself.

Perhaps, you might consider exploring page numbering, headers and footers, tables, frames, drawing, and outlining, in that order. We leave it to you. However, if you would prefer to be guided through these topics, then may we suggest you look up the later chapters of the book *Word 95 explained* (BP406), also published by BERNARD BABANI (publishing) Ltd.

* * *

6. THE EXCEL SPREADSHEET

Microsoft Excel is a powerful and versatile software package which, over the last few years, has proved its usefulness, not only in the business world, but with scientific and engineering users as well.

The program's power lies in its ability to emulate everything that can be done by the use of pencil, paper and a calculator. Thus, it is an 'electronic spreadsheet' or simply a 'spreadsheet', a name which is also used to describe it and other similar products. Its power is derived from the power of the computer it is running on, and the flexibility and accuracy with which it can deal with the solution of the various applications it is programmed to manage. These can vary from budgeting and forecasting to the solution of complex scientific and engineering problems.

Starting the Excel Program

Excel is started in Windows 95 either by clicking the **Start** button then selecting **Program** and clicking on

the 'Microsoft Excel' icon on the cascade menu, by clicking the Excel icon on the Old Office Shortcut Bar, or by clicking the 'Open a Document' icon on the Office Shortcut Bar and double-clicking on an Excel worksheet file. In the latter case the worksheet will be loaded into Excel at the same time.

The first time you use Excel you get the 'What's New' Help screen displayed. After that, to get back to this Help screen, use **Help, Answer Wizard** and type *what's new* in the Type Your Request box, then select What's New in Microsoft Excel 95. We suggest you spend a little time examining at least the first four options of this Help screen, shown overleaf.

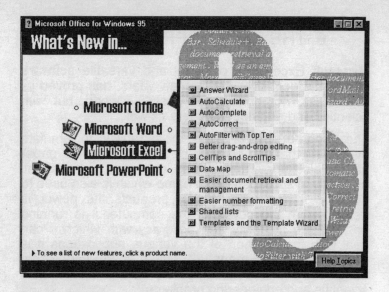

When Excel is loaded, a 'blank' spreadsheet screen displays with a similar Title bar, Menu bar, Toolbar and Formatting bar to those of Word. Obviously there are some differences, but that is to be expected as the two programs serve different purposes.

The Excel Screen

The opening screen of Excel is shown on the next page. It is perhaps worth looking at the various parts that make up this screen, or window, if only to see how similar it is to that of Word. Excel follows the usual Microsoft Windows 95 conventions with which you should be very familiar by now.

The window as shown takes up the full screen area available. If you click on the application restore button, the top one of the two restore buttons at the top right of the screen, you can make Excel show in a smaller window. This can be useful when you are running several applications at the same time and you want to transfer between them with the mouse.

68

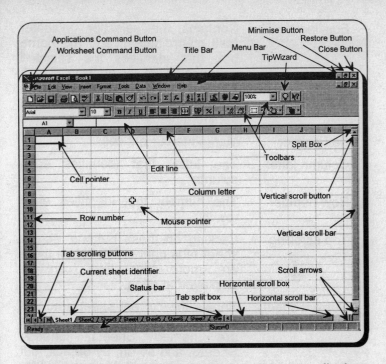

Note that the Excel window, which in this case displays an empty and untitled book (Book1), has some areas which have identical functions to those of Word (refer to 'The Word Screen' section in Chapter 2), and other areas which have different functions. Below, we describe only the areas that are exclusive to Excel.

Area	Function
TipWizard	The bulb icon which lights up if there is a quicker or more efficient way of performing the action you have just performed. Clicking on the icon displays the tip, while clicking on the icon once more removes it.

69

Edit line	Contains the selection indicator (cell co-ordinates), and the name box that identifies the selected cell, chart item, or drawing object. The edit line box can display a number, a label, or the formula behind a result.
Cell pointer	Marks the current cell.
Column letter	The letter that identifies each column.
Row number	The number that identifies each row.
Tab scrolling	Clicking on these buttons, scrolls sheet tabs right or left, when there are more tabs than can be displayed at once.
Current sheet	Shows the current sheet amongst a number of sheets in a file. These are named Sheet1, Sheet2, Sheet3, and so on, by default, but can be changed to, say, North, South, East, and West. Clicking on a sheet tab, moves you to that sheet.
Tab split box	The split box which you drag left to see more of the scroll bar, or right to see more tabs.

There is an extra split box on Excel's worksheet screen dump, which has not been identified. This is located at the extreme bottom-right corner of the screen, to the left of the 'right horizontal scroll arrow' button. The one identified on the screen dump is located at the extreme right of the screen above the 'top vertical scroll arrow' button. Both of these have to do with splitting the screen; the identified one horizontally, the other vertically. The use of both these split boxes will be discussed later.

Using Help in Excel

The Microsoft Excel Help Program provides on-line help in exactly the same way as the Microsoft Word Help program. You can use the **Help, Microsoft Excel Help Topics** command, then click the Contents tab, to obtain the following:

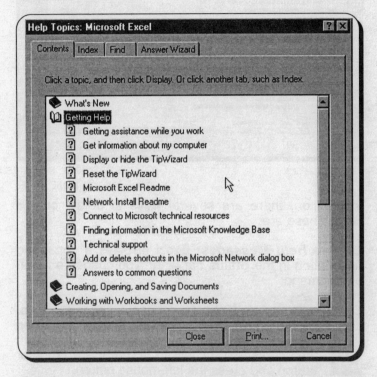

Help topics can be printed on paper by selecting the topic, then clicking the **Print** button.

Another way of obtaining help on a specific topic is to select the Answer Wizard, either by clicking its tab on the above window, or selecting it from the **Help** menu. You can then type your request in the top box and click the **Search** button, which lists the available information in the second box, as shown overleaf.

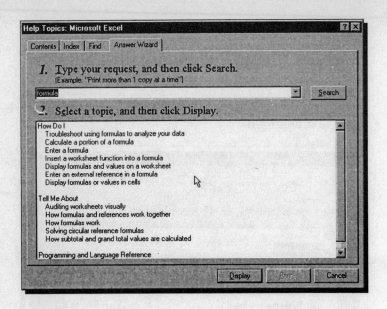

In addition, there are several ways to obtain on-line Help. These are:

On-line Help Messages: Excel displays a command description in the Status bar when you choose a menu or command.

Context Sensitive Help: To get context sensitive help, click the Help button on the Toolbar, shown here, then

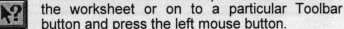 move the modified mouse pointer to an area on the worksheet or on to a particular Toolbar button and press the left mouse button.

Workbook Navigation

When you first enter Excel, the program sets up a series of huge electronic pages, or worksheets, in your computer's memory, many times larger than the small part shown on the screen. Individual cells are identified by column and row location (in that order), with present size extending to 256 columns and 16,384 rows. The columns are labelled from A to Z, followed by AA to AZ, BA to BZ, and so on, to IV, while the rows are numbered from 1 to 16,384.

A worksheet can be thought of as a two-dimensional table made up of rows and columns. The point where a row and column intersect is called a cell, while the reference points of a cell are known as the cell address. The active cell (A1 when you first enter the program) is boxed.

Navigation around the worksheet is achieved by using one of the following keys or key combinations:

- Pressing one of the four arrow keys (→↓←↑) moves the active cell one position right, down, left or up, respectively.

- Pressing the <PgDn> or <PgUp> keys moves the active cell down or up one visible page.

- Pressing the <Ctrl+→> or <Ctrl+↓> key combinations moves the active cell to the extreme right of the worksheet (column IV) or extreme bottom of the worksheet (row 16,384).

- Pressing the <Home> key, moves the active cell to the beginning of a row.

- Pressing the <Ctrl+Home> key combination moves the active cell to the home position, A1.

- Pressing the <Ctrl+End> key combination moves the active cell to the lower right corner of the worksheet's currently used area.

- Pressing the **F5** function key will display the Go To dialogue box shown below.

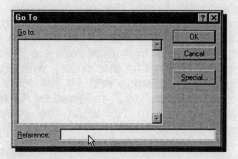

In the **Go to** box a list of named ranges in the active worksheet (to be discussed shortly) is displayed, or one of the last four references from which you chose the **Go To** command.

In the **Reference** box you type the cell reference or a named range you want to move to.

To move the active cell with a mouse, do the following:

- Point to the cell you want to move to and click the left mouse button. If the cell is not visible, move the window by clicking on the scroll bar arrowhead that points in the direction you want to move,

- To move a page at a time, click in the scroll bar itself.

- For larger moves, drag the box in the scroll bar, but the distances moved will depend on the size of the worksheet.

When you have finished navigating around the worksheet, press the <Ctrl+Home> key combination which will move the active cell to the A1 position (provided you have not fixed titles in any rows or columns or have no hidden rows or columns - more about these later).

Note that the area within which you can move the active cell is referred to as the working area of the worksheet, while the letters and numbers in the border at the top and left of the working area give the 'co-ordinates' of the cells in a worksheet.

The location of the active cell is constantly monitored by the 'selection indicator' which is to be found on the extreme left below the lower Toolbar of the application window. As the active cell is moved, this indicator displays its address, as shown below.

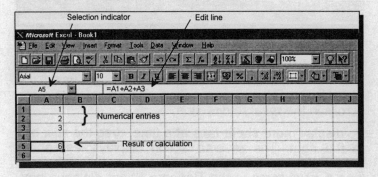

The contents of a cell are displayed above the column letters within what is known as the 'Edit line'. If you type text in the active cell, what you type appears in both the 'Edit line' and the cell itself.

Typing a formula which is preceded by the equals sign (=) to, say, add the contents of three cells, causes the actual formula to appear in the 'Edit line', while the result of the actual calculation appears in the active cell when the <Enter> key is pressed.

Moving Between Sheets:

You can scroll between sheets by clicking one of the arrows situated to the left of Sheet 1, as shown below. We have labelled these as 'Tab scrolling buttons'. The inner arrows scroll sheets one at a time in the direction of the arrow, while the outer arrows scroll to the end, or beginning, of the group of available sheets. A sheet is then made current by clicking its tab.

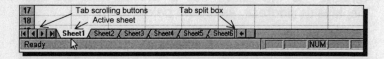

With the keyboard, you can scroll one sheet at a time, and make it active at the same time, by using the <Ctrl+PgDn> key combination. Using <Ctrl+PgUp> scrolls in the reverse direction.

To display more sheet tabs at a time, drag the split box to the right. The reverse action displays less sheet tabs. To rename sheets, double-click at their tab, then type a new name in the Rename Sheet dialogue box, as shown below.

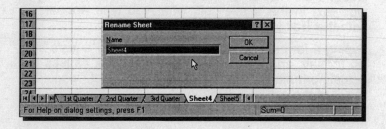

To insert a sheet in front of a certain sheet, make that sheet current, then use the **Insert, Worksheet** command sequence. To delete a sheet, make it current and use the **Edit, Delete Sheet** command sequence.

Rearranging Sheet Order:

If you need to rearrange the order in which sheets are being held in a workbook, you can do so by dragging a particular sheet to its new position, as shown below.

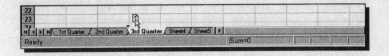

While you are dragging the tab of the sheet you want to move, the mouse pointer changes to an arrow pointing to a sheet. The small solid arrowhead to the left of the mouse pointer indicates the place where the sheet you are moving will be placed.

Grouping Worksheets:

You can select several sheets to group them together so that data entry, editing, or formatting can be made easier and more consistent.

To select adjacent sheets, click the first sheet tab, hold down the <Shift> key and then click the last sheet tab in the group. To select non-adjacent sheets, click the first sheet tab, hold down the <Ctrl> key and then click the other sheet tabs you want to group together.

Selecting sheets in the above manner, causes the word '[Group]' to appear in the Title bar of the active window, and the tabs of the selected sheets to be shown in white. To cancel the selection, click at the tab of any sheet which is not part of the selected group.

Shortcut Menus:

While a range of cells in a sheet is selected, or a group of sheets is active, you can access a shortcut menu of relevant commands by pressing the right mouse button. This produces a shortcut menu of the most common commands relevant to what you are doing at the time.

Viewing Multiple Workbook Sheets

To see more clearly what you are doing when starting with multiple workbook sheets, type the text '1st' in location A1 of 1st Quarter sheet, '2nd' in the 2nd Quarter sheet, and so on. Then use the **Window, New Window** command to add three extra windows to your worksheet, and the **Window, Arrange, Tiled** command to display the four sheets as shown below.

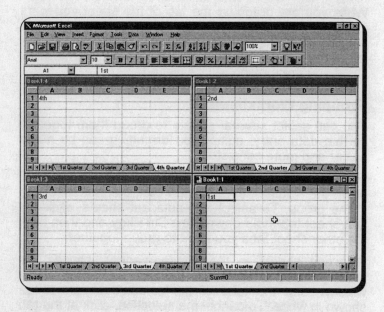

To move from one window to another, simply point with the mouse to the cell of the window you want to go to and click the left mouse button. To display a different sheet in each window, go to a window and click the sheet's tab.

To return to single-window view mode from a tiled or cascade mode, click the maximise button of the active window.

7. FILLING IN A WORKSHEET

Entering Information

We will now investigate how information can be entered into a worksheet. But first, make sure you are in Sheet1, then return to the Home (A1) position, by pressing the <Ctrl+Home> key combination, then type the words:

```
PROJECT ANALYSIS
```

As you type, the characters appear in both the 'Edit line' and the active cell. If you make a mistake, press the <BkSp> key to erase the previous letter or the <Esc> key to start again. When you have finished, press <Enter>.

Note that what you have just typed in has been entered in cell A1, even though the whole of the word ANALYSIS appears to be in cell B1. If you use the right arrow key to move the active cell to B1 you will see that the cell is indeed empty.

Typing any letter at the beginning of an entry into a cell results in a 'text' entry being formed automatically, otherwise known as a 'label'. If the length of the text is longer than the width of a cell, it will continue into the next cell to the right of the current active cell, provided that cell is empty, otherwise the displayed information will be truncated.

To edit information already in a cell, either

- double-click the cell in question, or
- make that cell the active cell and press the **F2** function key.

The cursor keys, the <Home> and <End> keys, as well as the <Ins> and <Del> keys can be used to move the cursor and/or edit information as required.

You can also 'undo' the most recent operation that has been carried out since the program was last in the **Ready** mode, by using the **Edit, Undo Entry** command.

Next, use the arrow keys to move the active cell to B3 and type

```
Jan
```

Pressing the right arrow key (→) will automatically enter the typed information into the cell and also move the active cell one cell to the right, in this case to C3. Now type

```
Feb
```

and press <Enter>.

The looks of a worksheet can be enhanced somewhat by using different types of borders around specific cells. To do this, first select the range of cells (as discussed below), then click at the down arrow of the Borders icon on the Formatting Toolbar, shown here, which displays a choice of twelve different types of borders, as shown below.

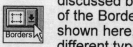

Selecting a Range of Cells:

To select a range of cells, say, A3:C3, point to cell A3, then

- press the left mouse button, and while holding it pressed, drag the mouse to the right.

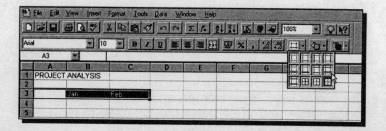

In our example, we have selected the cell range A3:C3, then we chose the 8th border from the display table.

To select a range from the keyboard, first make active the first cell in the range, then

- hold down the <Shift> key and use the right arrow key (→) to highlight the required range.

To select a 3D range, across several sheets, select the range in the first sheet, then

- release the mouse button, hold down the <Shift> key, and click the Tab of the last sheet in the range.

To continue with our example, move to cell A4 and type the label Income, then enter the numbers 14000 and 15000 in cells B4 and C4, respectively. What you should have on your screen now, is shown below.

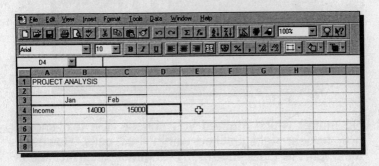

Note how the labels 'Jan' and 'Feb' do not appear above the numbers 14000 and 15000. This is because by default, labels are left justified, while numbers are right justified.

Changing Text Alignment and Fonts:

One way of improving the looks of this worksheet is to
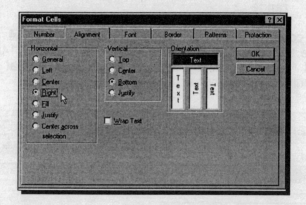also right justify the text 'Jan' and 'Feb' within
their respective cells. To do this, move the
active cell to B3 and select the range B3 to C3
by dragging the mouse, then either click the
'Align Right' icon, shown here, or choose the

   Format, **C**ells

command, then select the **Alignment** tab from the
displayed Format Cells dialogue box, shown below,
choose the **Right** button from the list under
Horizontal, and press **OK**.

No matter which method you choose, the text should
now appear right justified within their cells. However,
although the latter method is lengthier, it nevertheless
provides you with greater flexibility in displaying text,
both in terms of position and orientation.

We could further improve the looks of our worksheet by
choosing a different font for the heading 'Project
Analysis'. To achieve this, select cell A1, then click on
the 'Font Size' button on the second Toolbar, to reveal
the band of available point sizes for the selected font,
as shown overleaf. From this band, choose 14, then
click in succession the 'Bold' and 'Italic' icons.

Finally, since the numbers in cells B4 to C4 represent money, it would be better if these were prefixed with the £ sign. To do this, select the cell range B4:C4, then either click the 'Currency Style' button on the second Toolbar, shown here, or choose the

F̲ormat, S̲tyle

command and select **Currency** from the list under **S̲tyle Name** in the displayed Style dialogue box.

The numbers within the chosen range will now be displayed in currency form, provided the width of the cells is sufficient to accommodate them. In our example, the entered numbers are far too long to fit in currency form in the default cell width and appear as shown under the 'Feb' entry.

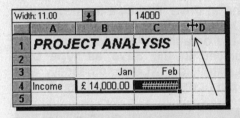

To see the actual numbers we must increase the width of the columns B4:C4 to 11 characters wide (as shown at the top left of the adjacent display). To do this, place the mouse pointer in between the column letters on the dividing line, and drag the pointer to the right, as pointed to above, until the width of the column is displayed as 11.00. The resultant worksheet should look as follows:

	A	B	C	D	E	F	G	H	I
1	*PROJECT ANALYSIS*								
2									
3		Jan	Feb						
4	Income	£ 14,000.00	£15,000.00	⇩					
5									

83

Saving a Workbook

Now, let us assume that we would like to stop at this point, but would also like to save the work entered so far before leaving the program. First, return to the Home position by pressing <Ctrl+Home>. This is good practice because when a workbook is opened later, the position of the cell pointer at the time of saving the file appears at the top left corner of the opened worksheet which might cause confusion if below and to the right of it there are no entries - you might think that you opened an empty worksheet.

Next, choose the

File, Save

command to reveal the Save As dialogue box, select to save your work in the **a:** drive, and type the new name of the file, say, **PROJECT 1** in the **File name** box. The file will be saved in the default file type *Microsoft Excel Workbook*, as displayed in the **Save as type** box. Excel adds the file extension **.XLS** automatically and uses it to identify it, but normally you cannot see it.

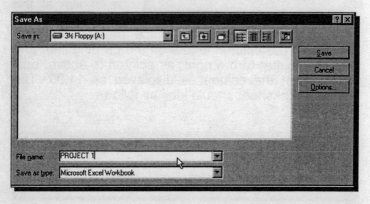

If you want to create backup files or provide password protection to your file, click the **Options** button. Clicking the **Save** button, causes the file to be saved under the chosen name.

Opening a Workbook

An already saved workbook, or file, can be opened by
either clicking at the 'Open' icon, shown here,
or selecting the

File, Open

command which displays the Open dialogue box. Do
not forget to change the drive to **a:**, if that is where you
saved your work (by selecting Floppy (A:) in the **Look
in** box drop-down list). Excel asks for a filename to
open, with the default *Microsoft Excel Files* being
displayed in the **Files of type** box. If the file was
saved, select it by clicking its name in the list box, then
click the **Open** button. If you haven't saved it, don't
worry as you could just as easily start afresh.

Next use the **F2** function key to 'Edit' existing entries or
simply retype the contents of cells (see below for
formatting) so that your worksheet looks as follows:

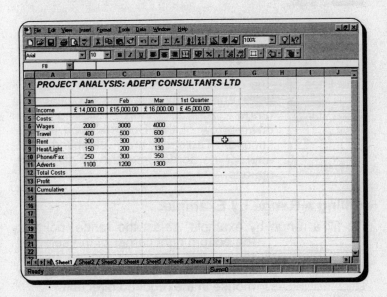

Formatting Entries

The information in cell A1 (PROJECT ANALYSIS: ADEPT CONSULTANTS LTD) was entered left justified and formatted by clicking on the 'Font Size' button on the Formatting Toolbar, and selecting 14 point font size from the band of available font sizes, then clicking in succession the 'Bold' and 'Italic' icons.

The text in the cell block B3:E3 was formatted by first selecting the range and then clicking the 'Centre' alignment icon on the second Toolbar, so the text within the range was displayed centre justified.

The numbers within the cell block B4:E4 were formatted by first selecting the range, then clicking the 'Currency Style' icon on the second Toolbar, shown here, so the numbers appeared with two digits after the decimal point and prefixed with the £ sign.

All the text appearing in column A (apart from that in cell A1) was just typed in (left justified), as shown in the screen dump on the previous page.

The lines, like the double line stretching from A3 to E3

were entered by first selecting the cell range A3:E3, then clicking the down-arrow of the 'Borders' icon on the second Toolbar, and selecting the appropriate border from the 12 displayed options.

Filling a Range by Example:

To fill a range by example, select the range, point at

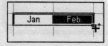

the bottom right corner of the selected range and when the mouse pointer changes to a small cross, drag the mouse in the required direction.

86

In the previous case, the next cell to the right will automatically fill with the text 'Mar' (Excel anticipates that you want to fill cells by example with the abbreviations for months, and does it for you). Not only that, but it also copies the format of the selected range forward. It is, therefore, evident that selecting ranges and using icons makes various tasks a lot easier.

Microsoft Excel allows you to format both text (labels) and numbers in any way you choose. For example, you can have numbers centre justified in their cells.

Entering Text, Numbers and Formulae:

When text, a number, a formula, or an Excel function is entered into a cell, or reference is made to the contents of a cell by the cell address, then the content of the status bar changes from **Ready** to **Enter**. This status can be changed back to **Ready** by either completing an entry and pressing <Enter> or one of the arrow keys, or by pressing <Esc>.

We can find the 1st quarter total income from consultancy, by activating cell E4, typing

   =B4+C4+D4

and pressing <Enter>. The total first quarter income is added, using the above formula, and the result is placed in cell E4.

Now complete the insertion into the spreadsheet of the various amounts under 'costs' and then choose the

   File, Save As

command to save the resultant worksheet under the filename **PROJECT 2**, before going on any further. Remember that saving your work on disc often enough is a good thing to get used to, as even the shortest power cut can cause the loss of hours of hard work!

Using Functions

In our example, writing a formula that adds the contents of three columns is not too difficult or lengthy a task. But imagine having to add 20 columns! For this reason Excel has an in-built summation function which can be used to add any number of columns (or rows).

To illustrate how this and other functions can be used, activate cell E4 and press the Function Wizard button shown here. If the function you require appears on the displayed dialogue box under **Function Name**, choose it, otherwise select the appropriate class from the list under **Function Category**.

Choosing the **SUM** function, inserts the entry SUM(number1,number2,...) in the Edit line. Clicking the **Next** button, causes the appearance of a second dialogue box, as shown in the composite screen dump below, which allows you to insert the range over which the function is to be effective.

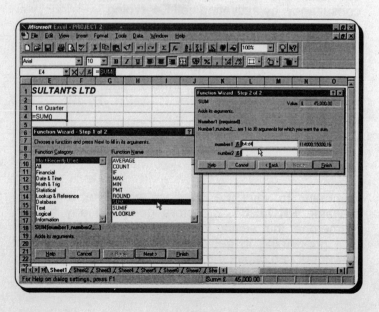

In this case, we enter B4:D4 and click **OK**, as the range we want to summate is continuous. If the range is not continuous, separate the various continuous portions of it with a comma (,).

Pressing <Enter> or clicking the **Finish** button causes the result of the calculation to appear in the active cell.

Using the AutoSum Icon:

With addition, there is a better and quicker way of letting Excel work out the desired result. To illustrate this, select the cell range B6:E12, which contains the 'Costs' we would like to add up. To add these in both the horizontal and vertical direction, we include in the selected range an empty column to the right of the numbers and an empty row below the numbers, as shown below.

Pressing the 'AutoSum' icon, shown here, inserts the result of the summations in the empty column and row, as shown below. The selected range remains selected so that any other formatting can be applied by simply pressing the appropriate icon button.

Now complete the insertion of formulae in the rest of the worksheet, noting that 'Profit', in B13, is the difference between 'Income' and 'Total Cost', calculated by the formula **=B4–B12**. To complete the entry, this formula should be copied using the 'fill by example' method into the three cells to its right.

The 'Cumulative' entry in cell B14 should be a simple reference to cell B13, that is **=B13**, while in cell C14 it should be **=B14+C13**. Similarly, the latter formula is copied into cell D14 using the 'fill by example' method.

Finally, format the entire range B6:E12 as currency, by selecting the range and clicking the 'Currency Style' button.

If you make any mistakes and copy formats or information into cells you did not mean to, use the

Edit, Undo

command which allows you to selectively undo what you were just doing. To blank the contents within a range of cells, first select the range, then press the <Del> key.

The worksheet, up to this point, should look as follows:

	A	B	C	D	E	F	G	H
1	PROJECT ANALYSIS: ADEPT CONSULTANTS LTD							
2								
3		Jan	Feb	Mar	1st Quarter			
4	Income	£ 14,000.00	£15,000.00	£ 16,000.00	£ 45,000.00			
5	Costs:							
6	Wages	£ 2,000.00	£ 3,000.00	£ 4,000.00	£ 9,000.00			
7	Travel	£ 400.00	£ 500.00	£ 600.00	£ 1,500.00			
8	Rent	£ 300.00	£ 300.00	£ 300.00	£ 900.00			
9	Heat/Light	£ 150.00	£ 200.00	£ 130.00	£ 480.00		⇩	
10	Phone/Fax	£ 250.00	£ 300.00	£ 350.00	£ 900.00			
11	Adverts	£ 1,100.00	£ 1,200.00	£ 1,300.00	£ 3,600.00			
12	Total Costs	£ 4,200.00	£ 5,500.00	£ 6,680.00	£ 16,380.00			
13	Profit	£ 9,800.00	£ 9,500.00	£ 9,320.00	£ 28,620.00			
14	Cumulative	£ 9,800.00	£19,300.00	£ 28,620.00				
15								

If everything is correct, use the **File, Save As** command to save it under the filename **PROJECT 3**.

Printing a Worksheet

To print a worksheet, make sure that the printer you propose to use was defined when you first installed Windows 95.

If you have named more than one printer in your original installation of Windows, and want to select a printer other than your original first choice, then select the **File, Print** command, click the down-arrow against the **Name** box on the displayed Print dialogue box and select the required printer, as shown below.

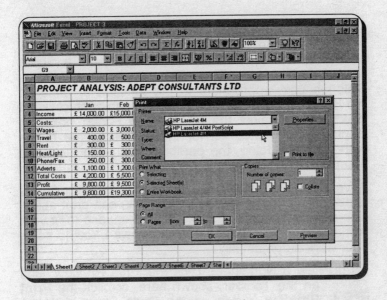

If you want to change the paper size, print orientation or printer resolution, click the **Properties** button on the Print dialogue box. These and other changes to the appearance of the printout can also be made by choosing the **File, Page Setup** command which causes the Page Setup dialogue box to be displayed, as shown overleaf.

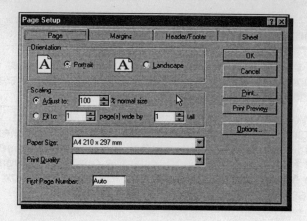

By selecting the appropriate Tab on this dialogue box, you can change your **Page** settings, page **Margins**, specify a **Header/Footer**, and control how a **Sheet** should be printed. Each Tab displays a different dialogue box, appropriate to the function at hand. In the **Header/Footer** dialogue box you can even click the down-arrow against the Header and Footer boxes to display a suggested list for these, appropriate to the work you are doing, the person responsible for it and even the date it is being carried out! Try it.

A very useful feature of Excel is the **Scaling** facility shown in the above dialogue box. You can print actual size or a percentage of it, or you can choose to fit your worksheet on to one page which allows Excel to scale your work automatically.

To preview a worksheet, click the 'Print Preview' icon 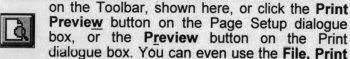 on the Toolbar, shown here, or click the **Print Preview** button on the Page Setup dialogue box, or the **Preview** button on the Print dialogue box. You can even use the **File, Print Preview** command!

The idea of all these preview choices is to make it easy for you to see your work on screen before committing it to paper, thus saving a few trees.

8. ADVANCED SPREADSHEETS

Enhancing a Worksheet

You can make your work look more professional by adopting various enhancements, such as single and double line cell borders, shading certain cells, and adding meaningful headers and footers.

However, with Excel you can easily select a pre-defined style to display your work on both the screen and on paper. To do this, place the active cell within the table (or range) you want to format, say C5, then select the **Format, AutoFormat** which will cause the following dialogue box to appear on the screen, displaying a sample of the chosen table format. In this way you can choose what best suits your needs. We selected 'Classic 2' and pressed **OK**.

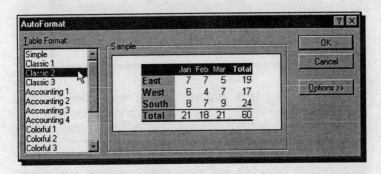

Next, reduce the title of the worksheet to PROJECT ANALYSIS, then centre it within the range A1:E1, by first selecting the range, then clicking the 'Centre Across Columns' icon, shown here, which causes the title to centre within the specified range.

Finally, save the worksheet as **PROJECT 4**, before going on.

93

Header and Footer Icons and Codes:

With the help of header and footer icons and their codes, shown below, you can position text or automatically insert information at the top or bottom of a report printout.

To add a header to our printed example, use the **File, Page Setup** command and click on the **Header/Footer** Tab, press the **Custom Header** button and type the information displayed below in the Left Section and Right Section of the Header box:

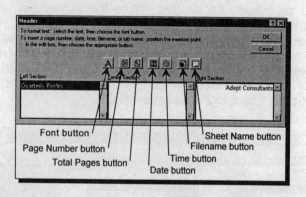

While the insertion pointer is in, say, the Centre Section of the Header box, pointing and clicking on the 'Sheet Name' button, inserts the &[Tab] code which has the effect of inserting the sheet name of the current active sheet at the time of printing. The first icon button displays the Font dialogue box, while the others display the codes listed below.

Code	Action
&[Page]	Inserts a page number.
&[Pages]	Inserts the total number of pages.
&[Date]	Inserts the current date.
&[Time]	Inserts the current time.
&[File]	Inserts the filename of the current workbook.

Setting a Print Area:

To choose a smaller print area than the current worksheet, select the required area by highlighting the starting cell of the area and dragging the mouse, or using the **<Shift+Arrows>**, to highlight the block, and use the **File, Print** command which displays the following dialogue box:

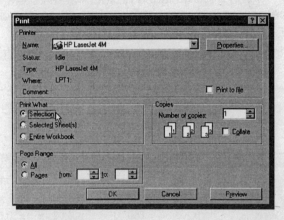

Choose the **Selection** button in the **Print What** box, and either click the **Preview** or the **OK** button to preview your report on screen or print it on paper. Once in preview mode, the following icons are available to you.

The first two allow you to change sheets, while the next one allows you to review your print output magnified or at full page size - when in full page size, the mouse pointer looks like a magnifying glass, as above. The next three icons can be used to print, change page settings, or to display and change the margins. To leave the preview option, press the **Close** button.

Another way to set the area to print is using the **File, Print Area, Set Print Area** menu command.

To print selected sheets or the entire workbook, click the appropriate button in the **Print What** box of the Print dialogue box.

The default selection in the **Print What** box is **Selected Sheet(s)** which is also what will be printed out if you click the 'Print' icon, shown here.

If you have included headers and footers, these will be printed out irrespective of whether you choose to print a selected range or a selected worksheet.

Printing our worksheet produces the following page:

Quarterly Profits				Adept Consultants
	Jan	Feb	Mar	1st Quarter
Income	£14,000.00	£15,000.00	£16,000.00	£45,000.00
Costs:				
Wages	£ 2,000.00	£ 3,000.00	£ 4,000.00	£ 9,000.00
Travel	£ 400.00	£ 500.00	£ 600.00	£ 1,500.00
Rent	£ 300.00	£ 300.00	£ 300.00	£ 900.00
Heat/Light	£ 150.00	£ 200.00	£ 130.00	£ 480.00
Phone/Fax	£ 250.00	£ 300.00	£ 350.00	£ 900.00
Adverts	£ 1,100.00	£ 1,200.00	£ 1,300.00	£ 3,600.00
Total Costs	£ 4,200.00	£ 5,500.00	£ 6,680.00	£16,380.00
Profit	£ 9,800.00	£ 9,500.00	£ 9,320.00	£28,620.00
Cumulative	£ 9,800.00	£19,300.00	£28,620.00	

5/1/96

Page 1

96

3-Dimensional Worksheets

In Excel, a Workbook is a 3-dimensional file made up with a series of flat 2-dimensional sheets stacked 'on top of each other'. Each sheet is the same size, and in itself, behaves the same as the more ordinary worksheets. As mentioned previously, each separate sheet in a file has its own Tab identifier at the bottom of the screen. Ranges can be set to span several different sheets to build up 3-dimensional blocks of data. These blocks can then be manipulated, copied, or moved to other locations in the file. A cell can reference any other cell in the file, no matter what sheet it is on, and an extended range of functions can be used to process these 3-dimensional ranges.

Manipulating Ranges:

The best way to demonstrate a new idea is to work through an example. We will use the worksheet saved under **PROJECT 4** (see end of previous chapter). Next, start Excel, use the **File, Open** command, or click the 'file open' icon, and select **PROJECT 4**. On pressing <Enter>, the worksheet is displayed on the screen as shown below.

	A	B	C	D	E	F	G	H
1		PROJECT ANALYSIS						
2								
3		Jan	Feb	Mar	1st Quarter			
4	Income	£ 14,000.00	£ 15,000.00	£ 16,000.00	£ 45,000.00			
5	Costs:							
6	Wages	£ 2,000.00	£ 3,000.00	£ 4,000.00	£ 9,000.00			
7	Travel	£ 400.00	£ 500.00	£ 600.00	£ 1,500.00			
8	Rent	£ 300.00	£ 300.00	£ 300.00	£ 900.00			
9	Heat/Light	£ 150.00	£ 200.00	£ 130.00	£ 480.00			
10	Phone/Fax	£ 250.00	£ 300.00	£ 350.00	£ 900.00			
11	Adverts	£ 1,100.00	£ 1,200.00	£ 1,300.00	£ 3,600.00			
12	Total Costs	£ 4,200.00	£ 5,500.00	£ 6,680.00	£ 16,380.00			
13	Profit	£ 9,800.00	£ 9,500.00	£ 9,320.00	£ 28,620.00			
14	Cumulative	£ 9,800.00	£ 19,300.00	£ 28,620.00				
15								

Projec~4.xls

Sheet1 / Sheet2 / Sheet3 / Sheet4 / Sheet5 / Sheet6

Copying Sheets in a Workbook

We will now fill another three sheets behind the present one, in order to include information about ADEPT Consultants' trading during the other three quarters of the year. The easiest way of doing this is by copying the information in Sheet1, including the formatting and the entered formulae, onto the other three sheets, then edit the numerical information in these appropriately.

To simplify this operation, Excel has a facility which allows you to copy a sheet into a workbook. There are two ways of doing this: (a) with the mouse, or (b) using the menus.

With the mouse, make the sheet you want to copy the current sheet, then press the <Ctrl> key, and while keeping it pressed, point with the mouse on the Tab of Sheet1 and drag it to the right, as follows:

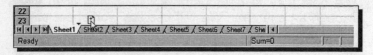

A small black triangle indicates the place where the copy will be inserted. If you insert a copy, say before Sheet2, when you release the mouse button the inserted sheet will be given the name Sheet1(2), as shown above, where we are about to insert a second copy before Sheet2 which will be named Sheet1(3).

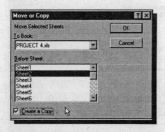

To copy a sheet with the use of menus, select the **Edit, Move or Copy Sheet** command, then highlight Sheet2 in the **Before Sheet** list of the displayed dialogue box, then check the **Create a Copy** option at the bottom of the dialogue box, and press the **OK** button. Sheet1(2) will be inserted in the Workbook, in the above case.

98

When you have three copies placed, double-click the Tabs of Sheet1 and the tree new sheets and change their names to 'Quarter 1', 'Quarter 2', 'Quarter 3' and 'Quarter 4', respectively.

The contents of the second sheet should be as follows:

	A	B	C	D	E	F
1	*PROJECT ANALYSIS 2nd Quarter*					
2						
3		Apr	May	Jun	2nd Quarter	
4	Income	£ 15,500.00	£ 16,000.00	£ 16,500.00	£ 48,000.00	
5	Costs:					
6	Wages	£ 3,500.00	£ 4,000.00	£ 4,500.00	£ 12,000.00	
7	Travel	£ 500.00	£ 550.00	£ 580.00	£ 1,630.00	
8	Rent	£ 300.00	£ 300.00	£ 300.00	£ 900.00	
9	Heat/Light	£ 150.00	£ 120.00	£ 100.00	£ 370.00	
10	Phone/Fax	£ 300.00	£ 350.00	£ 400.00	£ 1,050.00	
11	Adverts	£ 1,250.00	£ 1,300.00	£ 1,350.00	£ 3,900.00	
12	Total Costs	£ 6,000.00	£ 6,620.00	£ 7,230.00	£ 19,850.00	
13	*Profit*	£ 9,500.00	£ 9,380.00	£ 9,270.00	£ 28,150.00	
14	*Cumulative*	£ 9,500.00	£ 18,880.00	£ 28,150.00		
15						
16						
17						
18						

Quarter 1 \ **Quarter 2** / Quarter 3 / Quarter 4 / Sheet2

The easiest way to enter these 2nd Quarter results is to edit the copied data (from Quarter 1) by either using the EDIT key (**F2**), or double-clicking the cell you want to edit. You should now be in a position to complete editing this sheet. Be extra careful, from now on, to check the identification Tab at the bottom of the screen, so as not to get the sheets mixed up. You do not want to spend time editing the wrong worksheet!

After building up the four worksheets (one for each quarter - see page 104 at the beginning of the next chapter for details on the 3rd and 4th quarters) save the file as **PROJECT 5**.

Linking Sheets

A consolidation sheet could be placed in front of our 'stack' of data sheets to show a full year's results, by making a copy of the 1st Quarter sheet and placing it in front of it. Next, delete the entries in columns B to E, and name it 'Consolidation'.

We are now in a position to link the consolidation sheet to the other quarterly data sheets so that the information contained on them is automatically summarised and updated on it. The quarter totals in columns E of sheets Quarter 1, Quarter 2, Quarter 3, and Quarter 4, can be copied in turn to the clipboard using the **Edit, Copy** command, and then pasted to the appropriate column of the Consolidation sheet with the use of the **Edit, Paste Special** command and clicking the **Paste Link** button on the displayed dialogue box.

Note: Empty cells linked with this method, like those in cells E5 of each quarter, appear as 0 (zero) in the Consolidation sheet, and cannot be removed. To correct this, copy each column E of each quarter in two stages; E3:E4, then E6:E13.

Next, insert appropriate formulae in row 14 to correctly calculate the cumulative values in the Consolidation sheet. The result should be as follows:

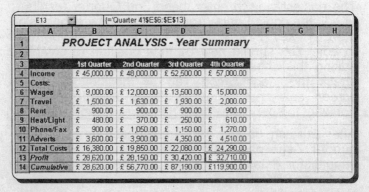

	A	B	C	D	E	F	G	H
	E13	▼	{='Quarter 4'!$E$6:$E$13}					
1		**PROJECT ANALYSIS - Year Summary**						
2								
3		**1st Quarter**	**2nd Quarter**	**3rd Quarter**	**4th Quarter**			
4	Income	£ 45,000.00	£ 48,000.00	£ 52,500.00	£ 57,000.00			
5	Costs:							
6	Wages	£ 9,000.00	£ 12,000.00	£ 13,500.00	£ 15,000.00			
7	Travel	£ 1,500.00	£ 1,630.00	£ 1,930.00	£ 2,000.00			
8	Rent	£ 900.00	£ 900.00	£ 900.00	£ 900.00			
9	Heat/Light	£ 480.00	£ 370.00	£ 250.00	£ 610.00			
10	Phone/Fax	£ 900.00	£ 1,050.00	£ 1,150.00	£ 1,270.00			
11	Adverts	£ 3,600.00	£ 3,900.00	£ 4,350.00	£ 4,510.00			
12	Total Costs	£ 16,380.00	£ 19,850.00	£ 22,080.00	£ 24,290.00			
13	Profit	£ 28,620.00	£ 28,150.00	£ 30,420.00	£ 32,710.00			
14	Cumulative	£ 28,620.00	£ 56,770.00	£ 87,190.00	£119,900.00			

Finally, save the resultant workbook as **PROJECT 6**.

Relative and Absolute Cell Addresses

Entering a mathematical expression into Excel, such as the formula in cell C14 which was

   =B14+C13

causes Excel to interpret it as 'add the contents of cell one column to the left of the current position, to the contents of cell one row above the current position'. In this way, when the formula was later copied into cell address D14, the contents of the cell relative to the left position of D14 (i.e. C14) and the contents of the cell one row above it (i.e. D13) were used, instead of the original cell addresses entered in C14. This is relative addressing.

To see the effect of relative versus absolute addressing, copy the formula in cell C14 into C17, as shown below:

C17	⬇		=B17+C16		
	A	B	C	D	E	F
1	*PROJECT ANALYSIS - Year Summary*					
2						
3		1st Quarter	2nd Quarter	3rd Quarter	4th Quarter	
4	Income	£ 45,000.00	£ 48,000.00	£ 52,500.00	£ 57,000.00	
5	Costs:					
6	Wages	£ 9,000.00	£ 12,000.00	£ 13,500.00	£ 15,000.00	
7	Travel	£ 1,500.00	£ 1,630.00	£ 1,930.00	£ 2,000.00	
8	Rent	£ 900.00	£ 900.00	£ 900.00	£ 900.00	
9	Heat/Light	£ 480.00	£ 370.00	£ 250.00	£ 610.00	
10	Phone/Fax	£ 900.00	£ 1,050.00	£ 1,150.00	£ 1,270.00	
11	Adverts	£ 3,600.00	£ 3,900.00	£ 4,350.00	£ 4,510.00	
12	Total Costs	£ 16,380.00	£ 19,850.00	£ 22,080.00	£ 24,290.00	
13	*Profit*	£ 28,620.00	£ 28,150.00	£ 30,420.00	£ 32,710.00	
14	*Cumulative*	£ 28,620.00	£ 56,770.00	£ 87,190.00	£119,900.00	
15						
16						
17			£ -			

Note that in cell C14 the formula was =B14+C13. However, when copied into cell C17 the formula appears as

=B17+C16

because it has been interpreted as relative addressing. In this case, no value appears in cell C17 because we are attempting to add two blank cells.

Now change the formula in C14 by editing it to

=$B$14+$C$13

which is interpreted as absolute addressing. Copying this formula into cell C17 calculates the correct result. Highlight cell C17 and observe the cell references in its formula; they have not changed from those of cell C14.

The $ sign must prefix both the column reference and the row reference. Mixed cell addressing is permitted; as for example when a column address reference is needed to be taken as absolute, while a row address reference is needed to be taken as relative. In such a case, the column letter is prefixed by the $ sign.

When building an absolute cell reference in a formula, it is easier to select the cell with the mouse pointer and keep pressing the **F4** key until the correct $ prefix is set.

Freezing Panes on Screen

Sometimes there might be too much information on screen and attempting to see a certain part of a sheet might cause the labels associated with that information to scroll off the screen.

To freeze column (or row) labels on a worksheet, move the cell pointer to the right (or below) the column (or row) which you want to freeze the labels on the screen, and use the **Window, Freeze Panes** command. Everything to the left of (or above) the cell pointer will freeze on the screen.

To unfreeze panes, use the **Window, Unfreeze Panes** command.

9. SPREADSHEET CHARTS

Excel allows information within a worksheet to be represented in graphical form which makes data more accessible to non-expert users who might not be familiar with the spreadsheet format. The saying 'a picture is worth a thousand words', applies equally well to charts and figures.

The package allows the use of several chart and graph types, including area, bar, column, line, doughnut, radar, XY, pie, combination, and several 3-D options of these charts. In all, Excel allows fifteen different types of charts, with a total of 102 pre-defined formats, which can be selected by using the appropriate icon. These are made available to you once you have selected the data you want to chart and indicated the place you want the chart to appear on your worksheet.

Charts (you can have several per worksheet) can be displayed on screen at the same time as the worksheet from which they were derived since they appear in their own 'chart' frame and can be embedded anywhere on a worksheet. Furthermore, they can be sent to an appropriate output device, such as a plotter or printer. Although this charting module rivals a standalone graphics package, and one could write a separate book on it, an attempt will be made to present its basics, in the space available.

Preparing for a Column Chart

In order to illustrate some of the graphing capabilities of Excel, we will now plot the income of the consulting company we discussed in the **PROJECT 6** file. However, before we can go on, you will need to complete the entries for the last two quarters of trading of the Adept Consultants' example, if you haven't already done so, as follows:

	Jul	Aug	Sep	Oct	Nov	Dec
Income	17,000	17,500	18,000	18,500	19,000	19,500
Costs:						
Wages	4,000	4,500	5,000	4,500	5,000	5,500
Travel	600	650	680	630	670	700
Rent	300	300	300	300	300	300
Heat/Light	50	80	120	160	200	250
Phone/Fax	350	380	420	400	420	450
Adverts	1,400	1,450	1,500	1,480	1,500	1,530

Next, link the quarterly totals to the consolidation sheet and calculate the year's total, and save as **PROJECT 7**.

	F6		=SUM(B6:E6)			
Projec~7.xls						
	A	B	C	D	E	F
1	**PROJECT ANALYSIS - Year Summary**					
2						
3		1st Quarter	2nd Quarter	3rd Quarter	4th Quarter	Total
4	Income	£ 45,000.00	£ 48,000.00	£ 52,500.00	£ 57,000.00	£202,500.00
5	Costs:					
6	Wages	£ 9,000.00	£ 12,000.00	£ 13,500.00	£ 15,000.00	£ 49,500.00
7	Travel	£ 1,500.00	£ 1,630.00	£ 1,930.00	£ 2,000.00	£ 7,060.00
8	Rent	£ 900.00	£ 900.00	£ 900.00	£ 900.00	£ 3,600.00
9	Heat/Light	£ 480.00	£ 370.00	£ 250.00	£ 610.00	£ 1,710.00
10	Phone/Fax	£ 900.00	£ 1,050.00	£ 1,150.00	£ 1,270.00	£ 4,370.00
11	Adverts	£ 3,600.00	£ 3,900.00	£ 4,350.00	£ 4,510.00	£ 16,360.00
12	Total Costs	£ 16,380.00	£ 19,850.00	£ 22,080.00	£ 24,290.00	£ 82,600.00
13	Profit	£ 28,620.00	£ 28,150.00	£ 30,420.00	£ 32,710.00	£119,900.00
14	Cumulative	£ 28,620.00	£ 56,770.00	£ 87,190.00	£119,900.00	
15						
16						

Consolidation / Quarter 1 / Quarter 2 / Quarter 3 /

Now we need to select the range of the data we want to graph. The range of data to be graphed in Excel does not have to be contiguous for each graph, as with some other spreadsheets. With Excel, you select your data from different parts of a sheet with the <Ctrl> key pressed down. This method has the advantage of automatic recalculation should any changes be made to the original data. You could also collect data from different sheets to one 'graphing' sheet by linking them as we did with the consolidation sheet.

104

If you don't want the chart to be recalculated when you do this, then you must use the **Edit, Copy** and **Edit, Paste Special** commands and choose the **Values** option from the displayed dialogue box, which copies a selected range to a specified target area of the worksheet and converts formulae to values. This is necessary, as cells containing formulae cannot be pasted directly since it would cause the relative cell addresses to adjust to the new locations and each formula would then recalculate a new value for each cell and give wrong results.

The ChartWizard

To obtain a chart of 'Income' versus 'Quarters', select the data in cell range A3..E4, then either click at the ChartWizard, shown here, or use the **Insert, Chart, On This Sheet** command. Once in the worksheet area, the cursor changes to a small column chart, as shown below.

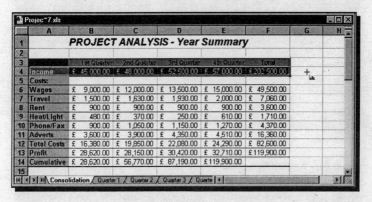

Now move the mouse pointer to the place you want to position the top-left corner of your chart, press the left mouse button and while keeping it pressed, drag the mouse down and to the right to form a dotted rectangle within which the chart will appear automatically once you release the mouse button and click the **Finish** button on the displayed ChartWizard dialogue box.

The result could be as follows:

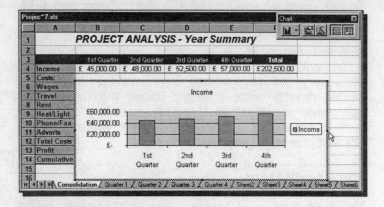

Note that while the frame containing a chart is selected

(you can tell from the presence of the small black squares around it), a special Chart toolbar, shown here, appears above and to the right of it. These icons have the following function:

 Produces a drop-down series of icons from which you can select the chart type.

 Allows you to select the default chart.

 Allows you to select ChartWizard's dialogue boxes to specify the data range for the chart and whether the data series is in rows or columns.

 Toggles the horizontal gridlines on or off.

 Toggles the legends on or off.

You can change the size of a selected chart by dragging the small four-headed arrow pointer (which appears when the mouse pointer is placed at the edges of the frame and on the small black boxes). You can also move the whole frame to a new position by clicking within it and dragging it to its new position.

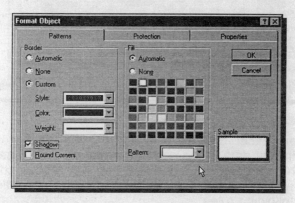

As an example of what you can do with a chart, let us select a pattern to be used as a frame, by using the **Format, Object** command and in the displayed Format Object dialogue box, shown above, select **Custom** under the Patterns tab and choose the 7th **Style**, the 4th **Weight** line, check the **Shadow** box and press **OK**. Next, click the Chart Type icon and select a 3D column chart, to obtain the displayed chart overleaf.

Try it, then change the first quarter income from £45,000 to £55,000 (on the Quarter 1 sheet), and watch how the change is reflected on the redrawn graph on the Consolidation sheet displayed on the next page.

Finally, revert to the original entry for the first quarter's income, change your chart back to a simple column type, and then save your work again under the filename **PROJECT 7** by simply pressing the Save icon shown here. Your current work will be saved to disc replacing the previous version under the same filename.

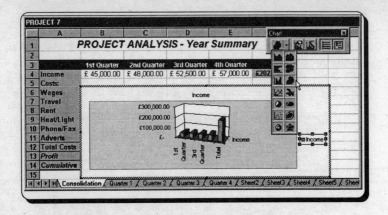

When Excel creates a chart, it plots each row or column of data in the selected range as a 'data series', such as a group of bars, lines, etc. A chart can contain many data series, but Excel charts data according to the following rules:

1. If the selected range contains more rows than columns of data, Excel plots the data series by columns.

2. If the selected range contains more columns than rows of data, or the same number of columns and rows, Excel plots the data series by rows.

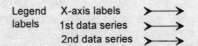

108

If you select a range to chart which includes column and row headings, and text above or to the left of the numeric data, Excel uses the text to create the axis labels, legends, and title.

If your data selection does not obey these rules, you must use the ChartWizard, and tell Excel how your data series is structured in the 4th displayed dialogue box. The ChartWizard opens 5 dialogue boxes altogether, as follows:

1. Range selection

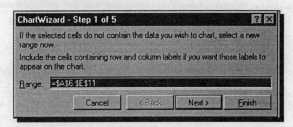

2. Chart type selection

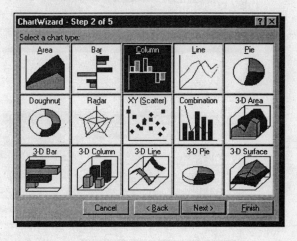

3. Format selection for chosen chart

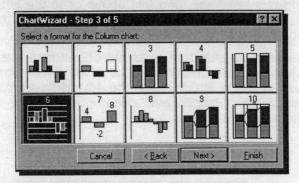

4. Data series specification

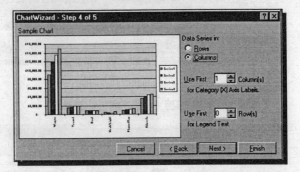

5. Legend and title selection

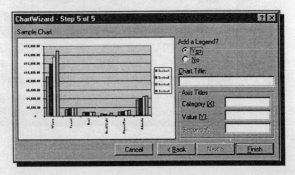

Saving and Naming Charts:

When you save a workbook, the chart or charts you have created are saved with it. Charts are numbered automatically as you create them and are given the default name **Chart #**, where **#** is a sequential number starting with 1. If you have created a chart and subsequently deleted it, the next chart created will be named one number above the deleted chart.

If you prefer, you can rename charts so that they have names more relevant to what they represent. To do so, select the chart by clicking within its boundaries, then click the Reference Indicator (above column A, which should display the name **Chart #**), type a new name and press <Enter>.

As we will be creating quite a number of charts, rename the existing **Chart 1** to **Income Bar**.

Pre-defined Chart Types

To select a different type of chart, click the ChartWizard icon shown here, or select the **Insert, Chart** command. The 2nd ChartWizard dialogue box displayed previously, lists 15 different chart options, but 6 of these are 3D versions of Area, Bar, Column, Line, Pie, and Surface charts. The nine main graph-types are normally used to describe the following relationships between data:

Area: for showing a volume relationship between two series, such as production or sales, over a given length of time.

Bar: for comparing differences in data - non-continuous data that are not related over time - by depicting changes in horizontal bars to show positive and negative variations from a given position.

Column: for comparing separate items - non-continuous data which are related over time - by depicting changes in vertical bars to show positive and negative variations from a given position.

Line: for showing continuous changes in data with time.

Pie: for comparing parts with the whole. You can use this type of chart when you want to compare the percentage of an item from a single series of data with the whole series.

Doughnut: for comparing parts with the whole. Similar to pie charts, but can depict more than one series of data.

Radar: for plotting one series of data as angle values defined in radians, against one or more series defined in terms of a radius.

XY: for showing scatter relationships between X and Y. Scatter charts are used to depict items which are not related over time.

Combination: for comparing different chart types or different scaling systems by overlaying different type of charts (up to a maximum of four).

You can change the type of chart by selecting one of the fifteen alternate chart types (including the 3D variations of Area, Bar, Column, Line, Pie, and Surface) from the 2nd ChartWizard dialogue box, pressing the **Next** button and choosing one of the pre-defined charts from the displayed selection, provided your data fits the selection.

Customising a Chart

In order to customise a chart, you need to know how to add legends, titles, text labels, arrows, and how to change the colour and pattern of the chart background, plot areas and chart markers, and how to select, move and size chart objects.

Drawing a Multiple Column Chart:

As an exercise, we will consider a new column chart which deals with the quarterly 'Costs' of Adept Consultants. To achieve this, first select the cell range A3:E3 then, while holding the <Ctrl> key down, select the costs range A6:E11, press the ChartWizard icon (or use the **Insert, Chart** command), and select the target area. The column chart of the 6 different quarterly costs will be drawn automatically, as displayed in the 4th ChartWizard dialogue box shown in the composite screen dump below. Note that the highlighting of the selected range actually disappears once the target area is defined.

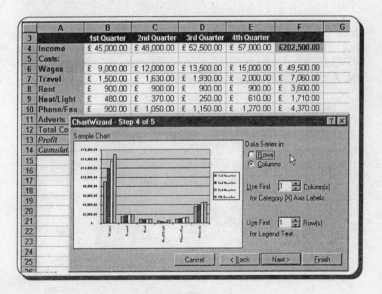

Because the selected range contains more rows than columns of data, Excel follows the 1st rule of data series selection which, however, might not be what you want.

To have the 'quarters' appearing on the x-axis and the 'costs' as the legends, we need to tell Excel that our data series is in rows by clicking the **Rows** button on the 4th ChartWizard dialogue box. Immediately this is done the column chart changes to:

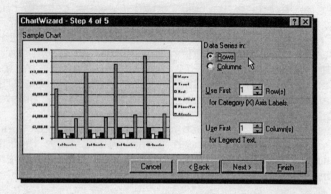

Now click the **Next** button, and type in the **Chart Title** box of the 5th ChartWizard dialogue box the heading 'PROJECT ANALYSIS - Year Summary', followed by the **Axis Titles** as shown below.

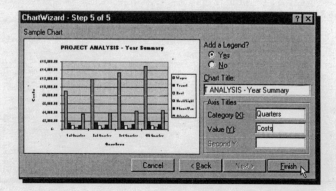

When you click the **Finish** button, the following chart appears on the screen:

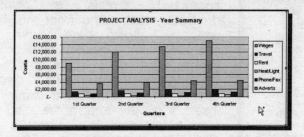

If you make a mistake and you want to try again, make sure the unwanted chart is selected, then press the <Del> key. Once you are satisfied with your efforts, name your chart **Costs Bar** and save your work under the filename **PROJECT 8**.

Changing a Title and an Axis Label:

To change a title or an axis label within a chart, double-click inside the chart. Once this is done, clicking at the title, the X- or Y-axis label, or the legends, reveals that these are individual objects (they are surrounded by small black squares) and you can edit or re-position them, or change their font and point size, as shown below.

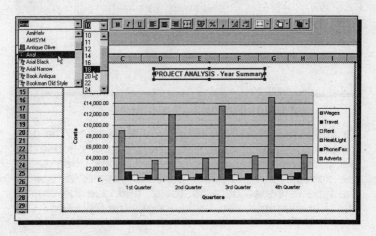

Once you have selected a chart, by double-clicking inside it, the **Insert** command reveals a changed drop-down sub-menu from the usual one, as shown here. From this sub-menu you can enter titles or axis labels, enter data labels, add chart legends, specify which axis to display, specify which gridlines to display, or insert a picture from a file. You can even select new data to add to your chart.

Drawing a Pie Chart:

To change the chart type, simply select the chart, then click the Chart Type icon on the **Chart** Toolbar and choose the pie picture from the displayed drop-down list. If the selected chart was the 'quarterly costs' chart, then on pressing the **OK** button the chart would be redrawn to the following:

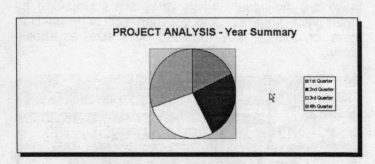

To obtain a different pie chart, you must select the data range again, then click the ChartWizard, choose the pie chart from the displayed chart types, then select the specific pie chart that best fits your data, specify the type of series data as 'rows', and give the chart a title. For example, you could choose the following:

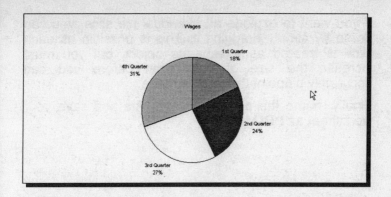

This chart tells us that Wages have increased from 18% for the 1st quarter to 31% for the 4th quarter, in a clockwise manner, but it doesn't tell us much more.

As a last example in chart drawing, we will use the data range A6:A11 and F6:F11 of the worksheet to plot a 3-D pie chart. The steps are the same as before, but for the 3-D option and specifying the type of series data as 'columns'. The result should be as follows:

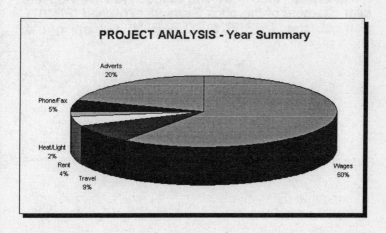

It is now obvious that the information contained in this chart is much more than in the 2-D version.

If you want to explode an individual pie slice, you can do so by simply dragging it. This is possible as each slice is treated as a separate object, but you must increase the size of your chart before you can accurately pinpoint the required slice.

Finally, name the pie chart **Costs Pie** and save your worksheet as **PROJECT 9**.

* * *

Excel has many more features than the ones we have introduced in this book. For example, you could use Excel's database and macro capabilities, and also explore its various tools, such as the Auditor, the Goal Seek, the What-if Tables, and the Solver. We hope we have given you sufficient basic knowledge to be able to explore these topics by yourself.

However, if you would prefer to be guided through these topics, then may we suggest you look up the later chapters of the book *Excel 95 explained* (BP407), also published by BERNARD BABANI (publishing) Ltd.

* * *

10. THE POWERPOINT ENVIRONMENT

Microsoft PowerPoint 95 is a powerful and versatile Graphics Presentation package which, however, is the least used of the MS-Office components.

The key element of PowerPoint is the Slide Show and the production of ancillary material, such as scripted notes to accompany each slide, laser copies of slides, and an outline view of all the information in the presentation. However, Microsoft uses the word slide to refer to each individual page of a presentation and you can format the output for overhead projector acetates, or electronic presentation on screen.

In addition, you can apply the skills you have already gained in using Word and Excel and use material created in these applications within PowerPoint.

Starting the PowerPoint Program

PowerPoint is started in Windows 95 either by clicking the **Start** button then selecting **Program** and clicking on

the 'Microsoft PowerPoint' icon on the cascade menu, clicking the PowerPoint icon on the Old Office Shortcut Bar, or by clicking the 'Open a Document' icon on the Office Shortcut Bar and double-clicking on a PowerPoint presentation file. In the latter case the presentation will be loaded into PowerPoint at the same time.

The first time you use PowerPoint you get the 'What's New' Help screen displayed. After that, to get back to this Help screen, use **Help, Answer Wizard** and type *what's new* in the Type Your Request box, then select What's New in Microsoft PowerPoint 95. We suggest you spend a little time examining at least the first four options of this Help screen, shown overleaf.

When PowerPoint is loaded, a screen displays with similar Title bar, Menu bar, Toolbar and Formatting bar to those of Word and Excel. Obviously there are differences, but that is to be expected as PowerPoint serves a different purpose to the other programs.

The PowerPoint Screen

The opening screen of PowerPoint is shown on the top half of the facing page. The program follows the usual Microsoft Windows conventions with which you should be very familiar by now. Scroll bars and scroll buttons appear within the window in which you load a presentation.

After clicking the **OK** button on the Tip of the Day box, the program displays the PowerPoint dialogue box, shown on the bottom half of the facing page. The options in this dialogue box make it easy for you to start your presentation.

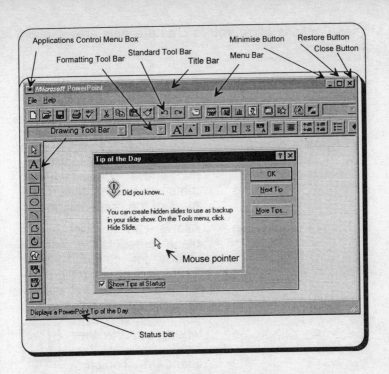

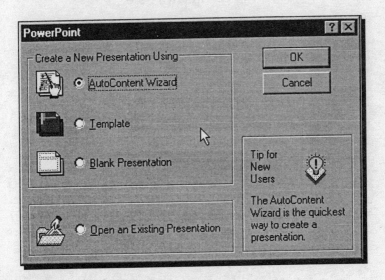

121

These options allow you to create a new presentation, as follows:

AutoContent Wizard   Activates a Wizard that helps you determine the content and organisation of your presentation.

Template   Allows you to select a presentation template that determines the colour scheme, fonts, and other design features of the presentation.

Blank Presentation   Allows you to start with a blank presentation with all values for colour scheme, fonts, and other design features set to default values. The same dialogue box also displays when you click the New icon on the Standard Toolbar, shown here.

The last option, at the bottom of the PowerPoint dialogue box, allows you to **Open an Existing Presentation**. Clicking this option, displays the File Open dialogue box which also displays when you click the Open icon on the Standard Toolbar, shown here.

From the File Open dialogue box, you can select where to look for your presentation files, or name a given presentation and let the program find it for you. You can even create a list of favourite presentations.

The only new item on the screen is the Draw Toolbar on the left of the display. It has the following functions:

	Selection Tool
	Text Tool
	Line Tool
	Rectangle Tool
	Ellipse Tool
	Arc Tool
	Freeform Tool
	Free Rotate Tool
	AutoShapes
	Fill Colour
	Line Colour
	Shadow On/Off
	Line Style
	Arrowheads
	Dashed Lines

To use these various tools, you must have a Presentation window open. The one shown overleaf is the Progress file which can be found in the **Wizards** folder which itself is in the **Powerpnt** folder.

Note the information given on the Status Bar at the bottom of the screen. In this particular case it tells you that you are looking at the first of nine slides, and that you are using the Default Design. There are two additional buttons on the Status Bar which allow you to add a New Slide, or change the Slide Layout. Also note the additional Slide View buttons above the Status Bar.

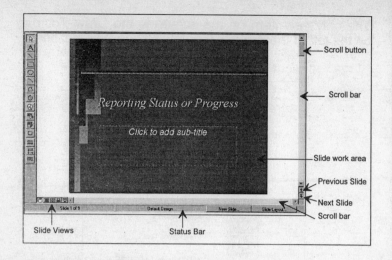

Scroll button

Scroll bar

Slide work area

Previous Slide

Next Slide

Scroll bar

Slide Views

Status Bar

PowerPoint Views

The Slide View bar at the bottom left corner of the Presentation window, is shown enlarged below.

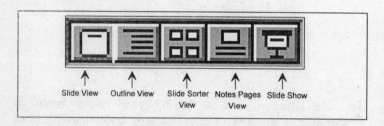

Slide View   Outline View   Slide Sorter View   Notes Pages View   Slide Show

These five Slide View buttons are the key to the editing power of PowerPoint. They allow you to replace the main Slide View edit window with an Outline View of the text which you can also edit. The Slide Sorter View displays thumbnail views of your work, and the Notes Pages View displays the notes page containing your scripted comments. Finally, the Slide Show view allows you to see your work as an electronic presentation on screen.

Outline View:

In Outline View, your work displays the slide titles and main text in typical outline mode. It is the easiest way of organising and editing presentation text.

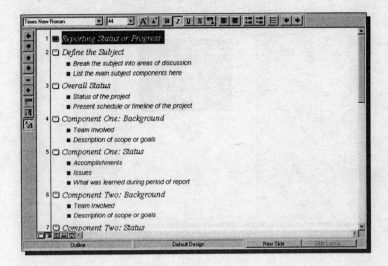

Slide Sorter View:

In this view, you can see the whole presentation at once. You can reorder slides, add transitions, and set timing for electronic presentations.

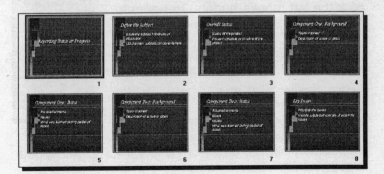

Notes Pages View:

This is where you create speaker's notes for any or all of your presentation slides.

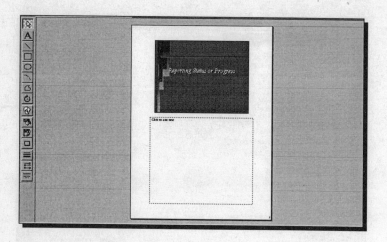

Slide Show View:

In this view you see your work as an electronic presentation, with each slide filling the screen. You can also see the effect of the transitions and timing that you set in the Slide Sorter View.

To see the next slide in full-screen view click the left mouse button. To return to a previous PowerPoint view from a full-screen Slide Show View, press <Esc>, or click the right mouse button to display the quick menu, shown here.

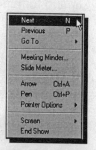

Finally, note that the Draw Toolbar options are sometimes different in different PowerPoint views. Their function is easy to learn; just point to each unfamiliar button in turn and a ToolTip will appear in a yellow box.

Using Help in PowerPoint

The Microsoft PowerPoint Help Program provides on-line help in exactly the same way as the Microsoft Word or Microsoft Excel Help programs. You can use the **Help, Microsoft PowerPoint Help Topics** command, then click the Contents tab, to obtain the following:

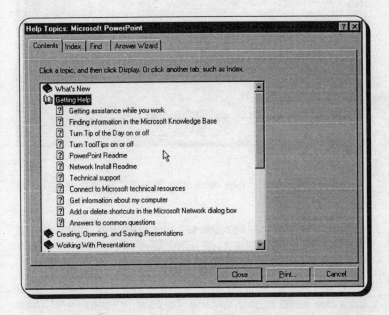

Help topics can be printed on paper by selecting the topic, then clicking the **Print** button.

Another way of obtaining help on a specific topic is to select the Answer Wizard, either by clicking its tab in the above window, or selecting it from the **Help** menu. Typing your request in the top box, and clicking the **Search** button, lists the information in the second box, as shown on the next page.

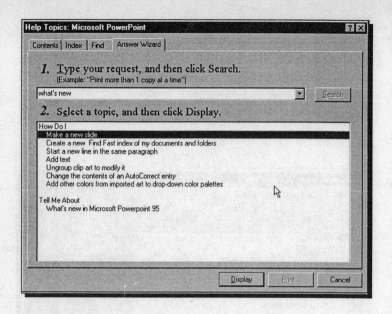

In addition, there are several ways to obtain on-line Help. These are:

On-line Help Messages: PowerPoint displays a command description in the Status bar when you choose a menu or command.

Context Sensitive Help: To get context sensitive help, click the Help button on the Toolbar, shown here, then move the modified mouse pointer to an area on the presentation or on to a particular Toolbar button and press the left mouse button.

11. DESIGNING A PRESENTATION

In this chapter we will use PowerPoint's Wizards to design a simple presentation quickly and effectively. Below, we show the first page of the finished presentation in black and white overhead format, so that you can have an idea of the overall design.

The AutoContent Wizard

When you first start PowerPoint, you are offered the opportunity to use the Wizard, select a template on which to base your work, or begin with a blank presentation.

Most users would, without question, like to produce a presentation in no time at all. The **AutoContent Wizard** is an excellent starting point, even if you know what you want to do and how to do it. Therefore, select it in the opening PowerPoint dialogue box, shown on page 121.

Later you can customise your presentation using PowerPoint's editing tools.

Clicking the **OK** button, starts the display of six dialogue boxes in which you are:

- Welcomed to the PowerPoint Wizards.

- Asked to specify what you are going to talk about (we typed the text *The PowerPoint Wizard*).

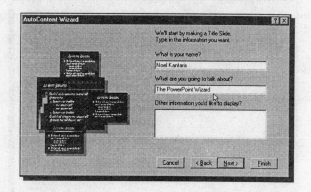

- Asked to select the type of presentation you are going to give (we selected *Training*).

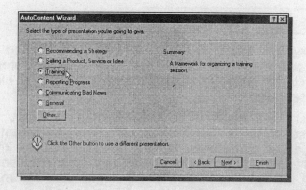

- Asked to select the visual style for the presentation (we selected *Default*).

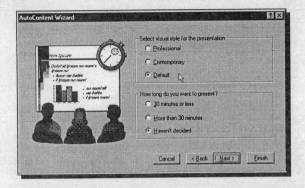

- Asked to select the type of output to be used (we selected *Black and white overheads*).

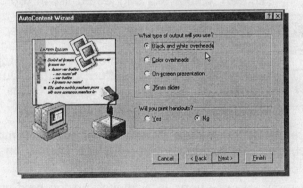

- Informed that your presentation is ready, and that you can replace suggested items at will.

When you click the **Finish** button of the 6th dialogue box, the AutoContent Wizard displays the first slide of the selected default set, as shown overleaf.

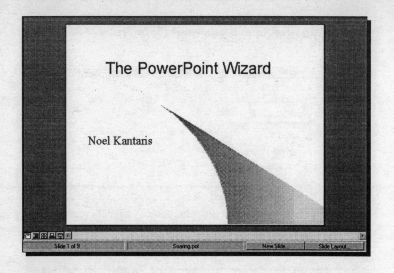

Clicking the Slide View button at the bottom of the screen, displays a suggested list of topics in Outline mode. We have used the usual editing methods (see Chapter 4) to replace some of these topics with our own, added some extra demoted (more indented) topics using the Demote button on the Outline Toolbar, shown here, and deleted topics that were of no relevance to our presentation.

To return to the original bulleted level from a demoted level, you have to use the Promote button on the Outline Toolbar.

The result of our efforts is displayed on the next page. Note that each numbered topic in the Outline mode, results in a different slide. These can be viewed by clicking the double arrow buttons at the extreme bottom right part of the window.

Save the result of your work so far under the filename **TRAINING 1**. Next time you open this file it will display in colour. To revert to black and white, click the B&W View button shown here.

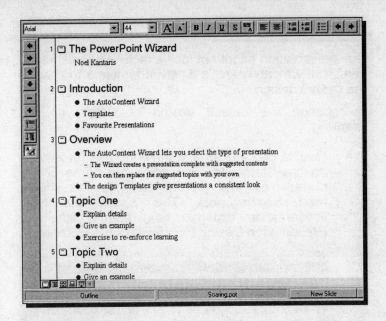

Clicking the Slide Sorter View button at the bottom of
the screen, displays all the slides in your presentation,
as follows:

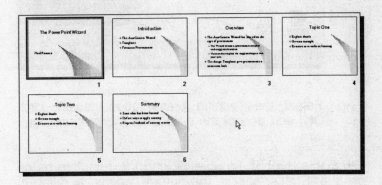

The order of the slides can be changed by simply left-
clicking at a slide and dragging the modified pointer to
its new position.

Selecting a Template

Our presentation might not look exactly what we had in mind, but we can select a different template to change the overall design.

To change the default design of slides, do the following:

- Double-click the area at the bottom of the screen on the Status bar that holds the name of the current template (in our example this should read **Soaring.pot**). This opens the New Presentation dialogue box, and clicking the Presentation Design tab, displays the following:

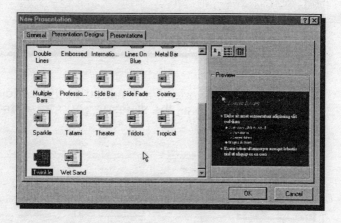

- Select the Twinkle presentation design, click **OK**, and accept the default on the next dialogue box.

Once this is done, double-clicking the template name on the Status bar in the future, opens a different dialogue box called Apply Design Template from which you can apply a different design template to your presentation. The above dialogue box only displays when you start a new presentation.

What appears on your screen now is the following:

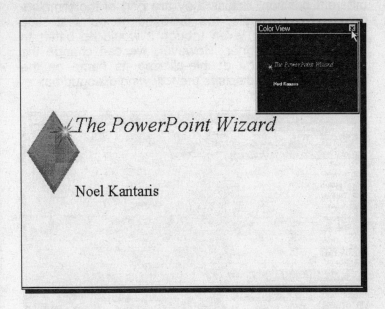

If you were working with a black and white presentation, what displays on your screen is in black and white, but in one corner of it you are given a taste of what this presentation looks like in colour. To remove this colour view, click its close button.

Adding a Drawing to a Presentation:

You can use the Drawing Tools on the left of the PowerPoint screen to add to your presentation.

We used the Ellipse Tool, the Text Tool, and the Color Fill to produce the logo shown here, which we placed at the bottom right corner of the first slide of our presentation. You, of course, can use your drawing skills to produce your own logo. Save your creation under **TRAINING 2**.

Rearranging Items in a Presentation:

Items on a presentation slide can be moved to a different position, unless they are part of the template design. For example, the diamond on our first slide cannot be moved, even though it would be better to have it slightly higher. However, we can change the template design by double-clicking its name on the Status bar, which displays the following dialogue box:

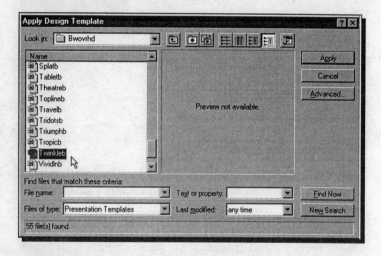

Selecting the Twinkleb template, gives us a slightly different position for the diamond on our presentation.

On the next page, we show the process of moving the main title from its present position to the new position of the diamond, as shown by the dotted rectangles. To achieve this, do the following:

- Point within the text area of the title and click the left mouse button. This causes a border to appear around the title.

- Place the mouse pointer on the title border and click the left mouse button. This places handles around the border, which can be used to increase the size of the border.

136

- To move the title, place the mouse pointer on the title border and drag it to the new position. The outer dotted rectangle indicates the border, while the inner dotted rectangle indicates the position of the text.

- Next, move the name of the presentation author to the bottom left corner of the presentation.

- Select this name by highlighting it and reduce the font size to 18.

These last two steps, reduce the prominence of the author's name on the slide, and allows a space to be created in the middle of the slide for the inclusion of a ClipArt object, to be discussed shortly.

Save the result of all these changes under the filename **TRAINING 3**.

Inserting a Clip Art Image

To personalise our work, let us insert a clip art image on the front page of our presentation. To do this, click the Insert Clip Art button on the Toolbar, shown here. This opens the Microsoft ClipArt Gallery, provided you have the means of accessing it, from which you can choose a picture.

Usually, the ClipArt Gallery is held on a CD-ROM disc because of its size. Note the different categories; there are 33 in all, each one of which has at least 25 images. We chose the first image of the first row of the Academic category.

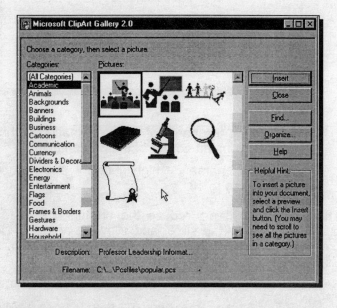

Clicking the **OK** button, transfers the image onto the title page of our presentation.

If you do not have access to the Microsoft ClipArt Gallery, you could always draw your own design.

Our final result (we will tell you what text enhancements to apply), is shown below.

To obtain the design shown above, do the following:

- Select the title text and click the Bold icon on the Toolbar. The title appears in italics as part of our choice of template.

- Insert a sub-title (we used *One step at a time*) at the position shown, select it and click the Bold icon on the Toolbar.

Save the final presentation as **TRAINING 4**. PowerPoint inserts the three letter extension **.PPT**, which however you cannot normally see, to distinguish such files from others in the Office suite.

In the future, double-clicking on this file in a My Computer or Explorer window, will open PowerPoint with the file active.

As an exercise, try to change the template of our presentation to that of Bludiagb, and change the first slide of it to the following:

* * *

PowerPoint is obviously capable of a lot more than we have introduced here, but you should now have the confidence to explore more of the package by yourself.

* * *

12. THE ACCESS DATABASE

Microsoft Access is a database management system (DBMS) designed to allow users to store, manipulate and retrieve information easily and quickly. A database is a collection of data that exists and is organised around a specific theme or requirement. It can be of the 'flat-file' type, or it can have relational capabilities, as in the case of Access, which is known as a relational database management system (RDBMS).

The main difference between flat-file and relational database systems is that the latter can store and manipulate data in multiple 'tables', while the former systems can only manipulate a single table at any given time. To make accessing the data easier, each row (or **record**) of data within a database table is structured in the same fashion, i.e., each record will have the same number of columns (or **fields**).

We define a database and its various elements as:

Database	A collection of data organised for a specific theme in one or more tables.
Table	A two-dimensional structure in which data is stored, like in a spreadsheet
Record	A row of information in a table relating to a single entry and comprising one or more fields.
Field	A single column of information of the same type, such as people's names.

In Access 95 the maximum size of a database is 1 gigabyte and can include linked tables in other files. The number of objects in a database is limited to 32,768, while the maximum number of fields in a table is limited to 255.

A good example of a flat-file database is the invoicing details kept on clients by a company. These details could include name of client, description of work done, invoice number, and amount charged, as follows:

NAME	Consultancy	Invoice	Value
VORTEX Co. Ltd	Wind Tunnel Tests	9601	120.84
AVON Construction	Adhesive Tests	9602	103.52
BARROWS Associates	Tunnel Design Tests	9603	99.32
STONEAGE Ltd	Carbon Dating Tests	9604	55.98
PARKWAY Gravel	Material Size Tests	9605	180.22
WESTWOOD Ltd	Load Bearing Tests	9606	68.52

Such a flat-file DBMS is too limited for the type of information normally held by most companies. If the same client asks for work to be carried out regularly, then the details for that client (which could include address, telephone and fax numbers, contact name, date of invoice, etc., will have to be entered several times. This can lead to errors, but above all to redundant information being kept on a client - each entry will have to have the name of the client, their address, telephone and fax numbers.

The relational facilities offered by Access, overcome the problems of entry errors and duplication of information. The ability to handle multiple tables at any one time allows for the grouping of data into sensible subsets. For example, one table, called client, could hold the name of the client, their address, telephone and fax numbers, while another table, called invoice, could hold information on the work done, invoice number, date of issue, and amount charged. The two tables must have one unique common field, such as client reference number. The advantage is that details of each client are entered and stored only once, thus reducing the time and effort wasted on entering duplicate information, and also reducing the space required for data storage.

Starting the Access Program

Access is started in Windows 95 either by clicking the **Start** button then selecting **Program** and clicking on the 'Microsoft Access' icon on the cascade menu, clicking the Access icon on the Old Office Shortcut Bar, or by clicking the 'Open a Document' icon on the Office Shortcut Bar and double-clicking on an Access database file. In the latter case the database will be loaded into Access at the same time.

When you start the Access program by double-clicking its icon, the following dialogue box is displayed on your screen:

From this dialogue box, you can either create a new database, or **Open an Existing Database**. If you select to create a new database, then you can select either to create a **Blank Database**, or use the **Database Wizard** to help you with the creation of the new database.

Access 95 makes extensive use of Wizards, which have been designed to help the new user to create databases more easily. In particular, the Database Wizard builds the necessary elements for 22 different databases for both home and business use. All you have to do is to answer a set of questions and the Wizard builds the database for you.

143

Parts of the Access Screen

Before we start designing a database, let us take a look at the Access opening screen. Below we also show the **what's new** help topic displaying its list.

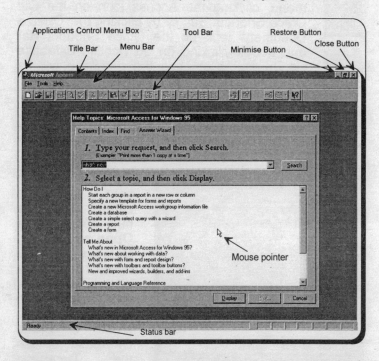

As you can see, these windows have some common screen elements with those of other MS Office applications. As usual, depending on what you are doing with Access, the items on the menu bar can be different from those of the opening screen. For example, once a database is opened the menu bar changes to the following:

Using Help in Access

The Microsoft Access Help Program provides on-line help in exactly the same way as the Help programs of the other MS Office applications. You can use the **Help, Microsoft Access Help Topics** command, then click the Contents tab, to obtain the following:

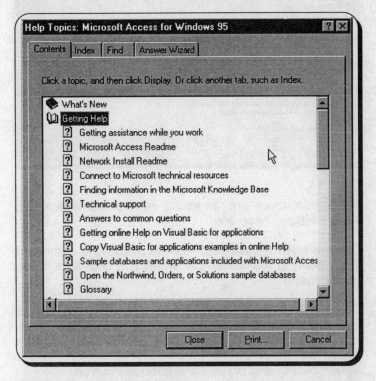

Help topics can be printed on paper by selecting the topic, then clicking the **Print** button.

Another way of obtaining help on a specific topic is to select the Answer Wizard, either by clicking its tab on the above window, or selecting it from the **Help** menu. You can then type your request in the top box and click the **Search** button, which lists the available information in the second box, as shown overleaf.

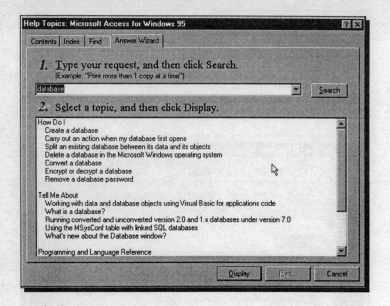

In addition, there are, as usual, several ways to obtain on-line Help. These are:

On-line Help Messages: Access displays a command description in the Status bar when you choose a menu or command.

Context Sensitive Help: To get context sensitive help, click the Help button on the Toolbar, shown here, then move the modified mouse pointer to an area on the presentation or on to a particular Toolbar button and press the left mouse button.

Database Elements

Before we start designing a database using Microsoft Access, it will be a good idea if we looked at the various elements that make up a database. To do so, start Access, which opens the simple, three-menu option Access screen with the **File**, **Tools** and **Help** options on the Menu bar.

Next, and if this is being done immediately after starting Access, select the **Database Wizard** option on 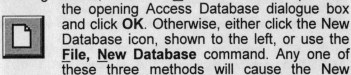 the opening Access Database dialogue box and click **OK**. Otherwise, either click the New Database icon, shown to the left, or use the **File, New Database** command. Any one of these three methods will cause the New Database dialogue box to be displayed, as follows:

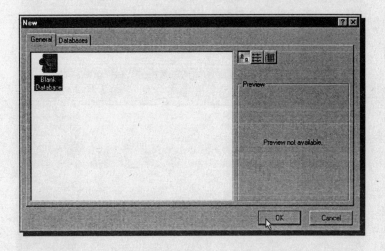

To create a new database, press the **OK** button. This opens the File New Database dialogue box shown on the next page.

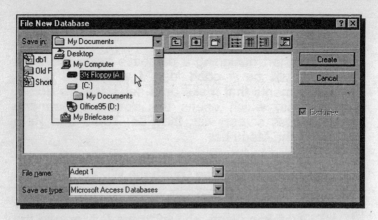

In the **File name** box, type the database name, say
ADEPT 1, which replaces the default name **db1**.
Access adds the extension **.MDB** which, however, you
don't normally see. We also decided to save this
example on floppy disc, therefore we clicked the down
arrow against the **Save in** box and selected the **3½"
Floppy (A:)** drive. Finally, pressing the **Create** button
displays the Database dialogue box as follows:

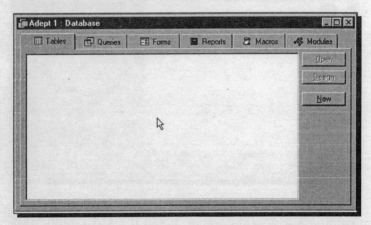

It is from here that you can design the various
elements that make up a database, such as Tables,
Queries, Forms, and Reports, all of which we will
examine in some detail in the next four chapters.

13. CREATING A TABLE

To design a database table, select the Tables tab and click the **New** button on the Database dialogue box, which displays the New Table, shown below immediately below the Database window. The first two options on the list, allow you to start designing a table from scratch, while the third option allows you to automatically select from a list of pre-defined table applications. The penultimate option allows you to import tables and objects from an external file into the current database, while the last option allows you to link a table in the current database to external tables.

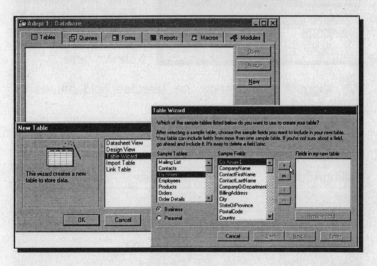

Selecting the third option and pressing **OK**, opens the Table Wizard dialogue box, shown at the lower right corner of the composite screen dump above.

The database we are going to create holds the invoicing details which the firm Adept Consultants keep on their clients. One table will hold the details of the clients, while another will hold the actual invoice details.

Choose 'Customers' from the **Sample Tables** list of the Table Wizard dialogue box, to reveal a list of appropriate fields for that table.

You can either select all the fields or you can select a few. For our example, we selected the following fields: CustomerID, CompanyName, BillingAddress, City, StateOrProvince, PostalCode, ContactTitle, PhoneNumber, FaxNumber and Notes, by highlighting each in turn and pressing the 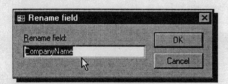 button.

Don't worry if these field names are not exactly what you want, as they can be easily changed. To change field names, highlight them in turn in the 'Fields in my new table' list and click the **Rename Field** button to reveal the Rename field dialogue box shown here.

We suggest you change the selected field names to those listed below.

CustomerID	CustomerID
CompanyName	Name
BillingAddress	Address
City	Town
StateOrProvince	County
PostalCode	PostCode
ContactTitle	Contact
PhoneNumber	Phone
FaxNumber	Fax
Notes	Order

When you have completed renaming the field names, press the **Finish** button, which displays the Customers Table ready for you to enter information.

To redesign the table, including changing its field

names, click the Design View icon shown here, or use the **View, Table Design** command. The following Table is displayed.

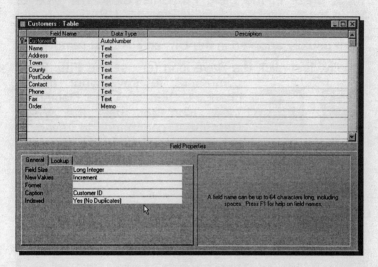

As each field name is highlighted, a Field Properties box appears at the bottom of the screen. If you were using this Table View to rename fields, then you should also edit the name appearing against the Caption property, or remove it altogether.

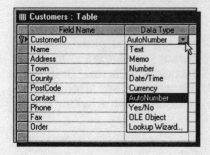

Next, place the cursor at the end of the Data Type descriptor of the CustomerID field which causes a down-arrow button to be displayed. Clicking this button, displays a drop-down list of data types, as shown here.

As we intend to use the first four letters of a company's name as the CustomerID field, change the current data type from Counter to Text. Similarly, change the data type of the last field (Order) from Memo to AutoNumber. Finally, place the cursor against the Phone and Fax fields and delete the entry against the Input Mask in the Field Properties box. The type of input mask displayed here is ideal for USA Phone and Fax numbers, but it does not correspond to the entry form usually adopted in the UK, so it is best removed.

Finally, first click the Save icon (or use the **File, Save**

command) to save your design changes, then click the Datasheet View icon (or use the **View, Datasheet** command) to revert to the Customers table so that you can start entering information, as shown below.

Customer ID	Name	Address	Town	County	Post Code	Contact
VORT	VORTEX Co. Ltd	Windy House	St. Austell	Cornwall	TR18 1FX	Brian Storm
AVON	AVON Construction	Riverside House	Stratford-on-Avon	Warwickshire	AV15 2QW	John Waters
BARR	BARROWS Associates	Barrows House	Bodmin	Cornwall	PL22 1XE	Mandy Brown
STON	STONEAGE Ltd	Data House	Salisbury	Wiltshire	SB44 1BN	Mike Irons
PARK	PARKWAY Gravel	Aggregate House	Bristol	Avon	BS55 2ZX	James Stone
WEST	WESTWOOD Ltd	Weight House	Plymouth	Devon	PL22 1AA	Mary Slim
GLOW	GLOWORM Ltd	Light House	Brighton	Sussex	BR87 4DD	Peter Summers
SILV	SILVERSMITH Co	Radiation House	Exeter	Devon	EX28 1PL	Adam Smith
WORM	WORMGLAZE Ltd	Glass House	Winchester	Hampshire	WN23 5TR	Richard Glazer
EALI	EALING Engines Design	Engine House	Taunton	Somerset	TN17 3RT	Trevor Miles
HIRE	HIRE Service Equipment	Network House	Bath	Avon	BA76 3WE	Nicole Webb
EURO	EUROBASE Co. Ltd	Control House	Penzance	Cornwall	TR15 8LK	Sarah Star

The widths of the above fields were changed so that all fields could be visible on the screen at the same time. To change the width of a

Customer ID	Name
VORT	VORTEX Co. Ltd
AVON	AVON Construction
BARR	BARROWS Associates
STON	STONEAGE Ltd

field, place the cursor on the column separator until the cursor changes to the vertical split arrow, then drag the column separator to the right or left, to increase or decrease the width of the field.

Sorting a Database Table

As you enter information into a database table, you might elect to change the field headings by clicking the Design Table icon and editing a field name, say from Name to CompanyName. If you do this, on return to the Customers table you will find that the records have sorted automatically in ascending order of the entries of the field in which you left the cursor while in the Design Table.

Contact	Phone	Fax	Order
Brian Storm	01776-223344	01776-224466	1
John Waters	01657-113355	01657-221133	2
Mandy Brown	01554-664422	01554-663311	3
Mike Irons	01765-234567	01765-232332	4
James Stone	01534-987654	01534-984567	5
Mary Slim	01234-667755	01234-669988	6
Peter Summers	01432-746523	01432-742266	7
Adam Smith	01336-997755	01336-996644	8
Richard Glazer	01123-654321	01123-651234	9
Trevor Miles	01336-010107	01336-010109	10
Nicole Webb	01875-558822	01875-552288	11
Sarah Star	01736-098765	01736-098567	12
			(AutoNumber)

If you want to preserve the order in which you entered your data, then sort by the last field (Order) with its type as AutoNumber. This can be done at any time, even after you finished entering all other information in your table.

Sorting a database table in ascending order of an AutoNumber type field, results in the database table displaying in the order in which the data was originally entered in that table. Above, we show the Contact field, so that you can cross-check the original order of your Customer table, as well as the rest of the information in that table not shown in the screen dump of the previous page.

To sort a database table in ascending or descending order of the entries of any field, place the cursor in the required field and click the Sort Ascending or Sort Descending icon, shown here.

With the keyboard, select the **Records, Sort** command, then choose either the **Ascending** or the **Descending** option.

Applying a Filter to a Sort:

If you would like to sort and display only records that fit selected criteria, use the **Records, Filter, Advanced Filter/Sort** command, which opens the Filter dialogue box, shown below.

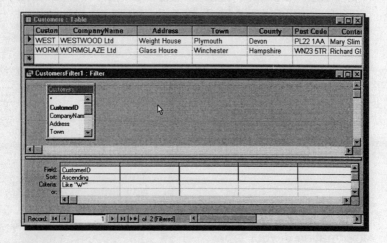

The upper portion of the dialogue box displays all the fields in the Customers table, while the lower portion is where you enter your filter restrictions. In the above example, we chose to view, in ascending order, the records within the CustomersID field that start with W - we typed W* and Access displayed *Like "W*"*.

On pressing the Apply Filter icon, the Customers table displays with only two entries, as seen in the above composite screen dump. To revert to the display of all the records, click the same icon again, which now appears on the Toolbar depressed, and bears the name Remove Filter.

Using a Database Form

Once a table has been selected from the Database window, clicking the down-arrow against the New Object button and selecting AutoForm, automatically displays each record of that table in form view. The created form for the Customers table is shown below.

Forms can be used to enter, change or view data. They are mainly used to improve the way in which data is displayed on the screen.

Forms can also be used to sort records in a database table in ascending or descending order of a selected field.

When you attempt to close a new Form window, you will be asked whether you would like to save it. An Access database can have lots of different forms, each designed with a different purpose in mind. Saved forms are displayed in the Database window when you press the Form button. In the above example, we chose the default name suggested by Access, which was Customers.

In a later chapter we will discuss Form design in some detail, including their customisation.

Working with Data

Adding Records in a Table: Whether you are in Table view or Form view, to add a record, click the New icon, shown here.

When in Table view, the cursor jumps to the first empty record in the table (the one with the asterisk in the box to the left of the first field). When in Form view, Access displays an empty form which can be used to add a new record.

Finding Records in a Table: Whether you are in Table or Form view, to find a record click the Find icon, or use **Edit, Find**. This opens the following dialogue box:

Custom	CompanyName	Address	Town	County	Post Code	Contact
AVON	AVON Construction	Riverside House	Stratford-on-Avon	Warwickshire	AV15 2QW	John Waters
BARR	BARROWS Associates	Barrows House	Bodmin	Cornwall	PL22 1XE	Mandy Brown
EALI	EALING Engines Design	Engine House	Taunton	Somerset	TN17 3RT	Trevor Miles
EURO	EUROBASE Co. Ltd	Control House	Penzance	Cornwall	TR15 8LK	Sarah Star
GLOW	GLOWORM Ltd	Light House	Brighton	Sussex	BR87 4DD	Peter Summe
HIRE	HIRE Servi					Nicole Webb
PARK	PARKWA'					James Stone
SILV	SILVERSN					Adam Smith
STON	STONEAG					Mike Irons
VORT	VORTEX C					Brian Storm
WEST	WESTWO					Mary Slim
WORM	WORMGL					Richard Glaze

Find in field: 'Customer ID'

Find What: `w*`

Search: All

☐ Match Case
☐ Search Fields As Formatted
☑ Search Only Current Field

Match: Whole Field

Find First
Find Next
Close

Note the field name on the Title bar, which is CustomerID, indicating that the cursor was in the CustomerID field before we clicked the Find icon or selected the **Find** command.

To find all the records starting with **w**, we type **w*** in the **Find What** box of the dialogue box. If the **Search Only Current Field** box is ticked, the search is carried out in that field. Pressing the **Find First** button, highlights the first record with the CustomerID 'WEST'. Pressing the **Find Next** button, highlights the next record that matches our selected criteria.

Deleting Records from a Table: To delete a record when in Table view, point to the box to the left of the record to highlight the entire record, as shown below, then press the <Del> key.

	WEST	WESTWOOD Ltd	Weight House	Plymouth	Devon	PL22 1AA
▶	WORM	WORMGLAZE Ltd	Glass House	Winchester	Hampshire	WN23 5TR
*						

To delete a record when in Form view, first display the record you want to delete, then use the **Edit, Select Record** command to select the whole record, and press the <Del> key.

In both cases you will be given a warning and you will be asked to confirm your decision.

Delete, Insert, and Move Fields in a Table: To delete

a field from a table, close any forms that might be open, then load the table from the Database window, then press the Design View icon, click the row selector to highlight the field you want to remove, as shown below, and press the Delete Row icon, shown here, or use the **Edit, Delete Row** command.

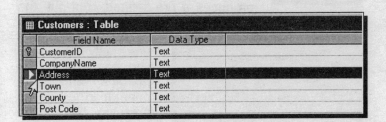

⊞ Customers : Table		
Field Name	Data Type	
🔑 CustomerID	Text	
CompanyName	Text	
▶ Address	Text	
Town	Text	
County	Text	
Post Code	Text	

To insert a field in a table, display the table in Design View, and highlight the field above which you want to insert the new field, and press the Insert Row icon, shown here, or use the **Insert, Field** command.

157

To move a field from its current to a new position in a table, select the field you want to move, then point to the row selector so that the mouse pointer is inclined as shown below, and drag the row to its new position.

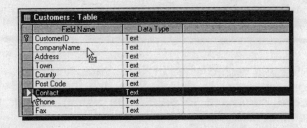

Note that while you are dragging the field, the mouse pointer changes to the one pointing at the Name field in the above composite. Releasing the mouse button, moves the Contact field to where the CompanyName field is now and pushes all other fields one row down.

Printing a Table View:

You can print a database table by clicking the Print icon, or you can preview it on screen by clicking the Preview icon.

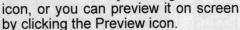
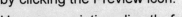

However, printing directly from here, produces a pre-defined print-out, the format of which you cannot control effectively. Although you can control the margins and print orientation by pressing the **Setup** or **Properties** button, you cannot control the printed font size.

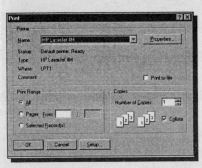

For a better method of producing a printed output, see the Report Design section.

14. RELATIONAL DATABASE DESIGN

In order to be able to discuss relational databases, we will add to the database of the previous chapter an Orders table. To do this go through the following steps.

- Open the **ADEPT 1** database and use the **New** button on the Database window to add an Orders table to it.

- Use the Table Wizard and select Orders from the displayed **Sample Tables** list. Next, select the five fields displayed below under **Fields in my new table** from the **Sample Fields** list, and press the **Next** button.

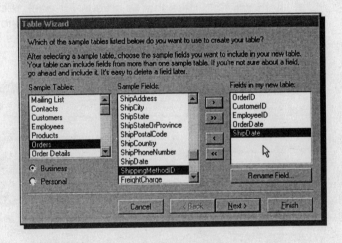

This displays the top dialogue box on the next page, in which you can, if you want to, change the name of the table. We selected to accept the default name, but we clicked the 'No, I'll set the primary key' radio button before pressing the **Next** key.

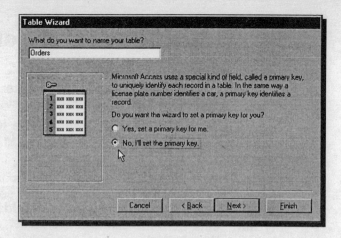

- On the next dialogue box you can select which field will hold data that is unique for each record. The key field must be unique in a table, and the OrderID field satisfies this requirement. This field is used by Access for fast searches.

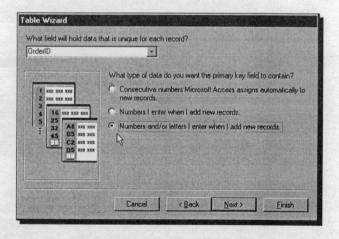

- Click the **Numbers and/or letters I enter when I add new records** radio button, before you press the **Next** button.

On the next dialogue box you specify whether the new table is related to any other tables in the database. The default is that it is not related.

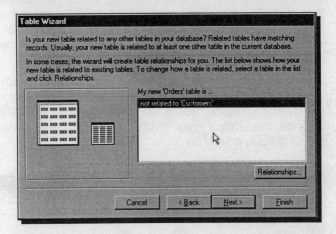

- Accept the default option, and press the **Next** button to reveal the final dialogue box.

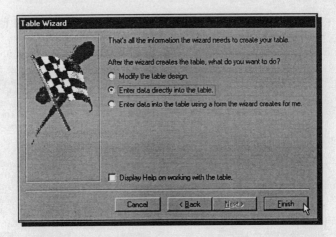

- Select the second option and press the **Finish** button, to let the Wizard create your table.

Although the two tables are actually related, we chose at this stage to tell the Wizard that they are not. This might appear to you as odd, but the Wizard makes certain assumptions about unique fields (for example, that ID fields are numbers), which is not what we want them to be. We choose to remain in control of the design of our database and, therefore, we will define the relationship between the two tables later.

The Wizard displays the newly created table ready for you to enter your data. However, before doing so, use the Design Table facility, as discussed previously, to change the Data Types of the selected Field Names to those displayed below.

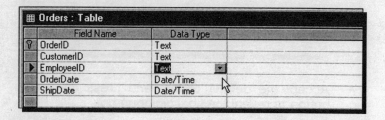

The information you need to enter in the Orders table is shown below.

Order ID	Customer ID	Employee ID	Order Date	Ship Date
94085VOR	VORT	A.D. Smith	20/03/95	10/04/95
94097AVO	AVON	W.A. Brown	25/03/95	14/04/95
94099BAR	BARR	S.F. Adams	01/04/95	02/05/95
95002STO	STON	C.H. Wills	20/04/95	25/05/95
95006PAR	PARK	A.D. Smith	13/05/95	16/06/95
95010WES	WEST	W.A. Brown	15/05/95	26/06/95
95018GLO	GLOW	L.S. Stevens	25/06/95	19/07/95
95025SIL	SILV	S.F. Adams	28/06/95	22/07/95
95029WOR	WORM	C.H. Wills	20/07/95	13/08/95
95039EAL	EALI	A.D. Smith	30/07/95	25/08/95
95045HIR	HIRE	W.A. Brown	18/08/95	08/09/95
95051EUR	EURO	L.S. Stevens	25/08/95	19/09/95
95064AVO	AVON	S.F. Adams	20/09/95	15/10/95

Record: 13 of 13

Relationships

Information held in two or more tables of a database is normally related in some way. In our case, the two tables, Customers and Orders, are related by the CustomerID field.

To build up relationships between tables, return to the Database window and press the Relationships icon on the Tool bar, shown here. This opens the following window in which the index field in each table is emboldened.

You can build relationships between tables by dragging a field name from one table into another. In our example below, we have dragged CustomerID from the Customers table (by pointing to it, pressing the left

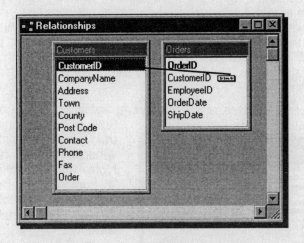

mouse button, and while keeping the mouse button pressed, dragging the pointer) to the required field in the other table, in this case CustomerID in the Orders table. Releasing the mouse button opens the dialogue boxes shown at the top of the next page (the second one by pressing the **Join Type** button on the first one).

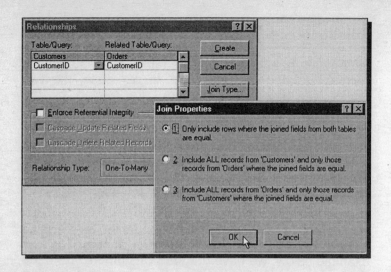

In the Join Properties dialogue box you can specify the type of join Access should create in new queries - more about this later. For the present, press the **OK** button on the Join Properties dialogue box, to close it, then check the **Enforce Referential Integrity** box in the Relationships dialogue box, and press the **Create** button.

Access creates and displays graphically the chosen

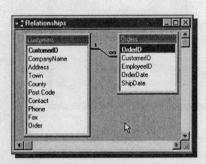

type of relationship in the Relationships window shown here. Note the relationship '1 customer to many (∞) orders' symbolism in the Relationships window.

Because Access is a relational database, data can be used in queries from more than one table at a time. As we have seen, if the database contains tables with related data, the relationships can be defined easily.

164

Usually, the matching fields have the same name, as in our example of Customers and Orders tables. In the Customers table, the CustomersID field is the primary field and relates to the CustomersID field in the Orders table - there can be several orders in the Orders table from one customer in the Customers table.

The various types of relationships are as follows:

- Inherited - for attaching tables from another Access database. The original relationships of the attached database can be used in the current database.

- Referential - for enforcing relationships between records according to certain rules, when you add or delete records in related tables belonging to the same database. For example, you can only add records to a related table, if a matching record already exists in the primary table, and you cannot delete a record from the primary table if matching records exist in a related table.

Viewing and Editing Relationships:

To view the current relationships between tables, activate the Database window and press the Relationships icon. This displays the following:

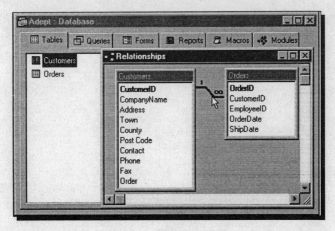

To edit a relationship, double-click the left mouse button at the pointer position shown on the previous screen dump. The tip of the mouse pointer must be on the inclined line joining the two tables in the Relationships window, as shown, before Access will respond. If you have difficulty with this action, first point to the relationship line and click once to embolden it, then use the **Relationships, Edit Relationship** command. Either of these two actions will open the Relationships dialogue box in which you can change the various options already discussed.

A given relationship can easily be removed altogether, by first activating it (pointing and clicking to embolden it), then pressing the <Del> key. A confirmation dialogue box will be displayed. To delete a table, you must first detach it from other tables, then select it in the Database Window and press the <Del> key. Think before you do this!

Creating an Additional Table

As an exercise, create a third table using the **Table Wizards** and select Invoices from the displayed **Sample Tables** list. Next, select the five fields displayed below - the names and their data types have been changed using the Design Table facility.

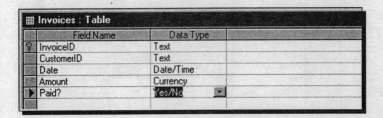

Field Name	Data Type
InvoiceID	Text
CustomerID	Text
Date	Date/Time
Amount	Currency
Paid?	Yes/No

Next, enter the data given below and build up appropriate relationships between the Invoices table, the Customers table and the Orders table, as shown on the next page.

Invoice No	Customer ID	Date	Amount	Paid?
AD9501	VORT	10/04/95	£120.84	☐
AD9502	AVON	14/04/95	£103.52	☑
AD9503	BARR	02/05/95	£99.32	☐
AD9504	STON	25/05/95	£55.98	☐
AD9505	PARK	16/06/95	£180.22	☐
AD9506	WEST	26/06/95	£68.52	☐
AD9507	GLOW	19/07/95	£111.56	☐
AD9508	SILV	22/07/95	£123.45	☑
AD9509	WORM	13/08/95	£35.87	☐
AD9510	EALI	25/08/95	£58.95	☐
AD9511	HIRE	08/09/95	£290.00	☐
AD9512	EURO	19/09/95	£150.00	☐
AD9513	AVON	15/10/95	£135.00	☐
				☐

The relationships between the three tables should be arranged as follows:

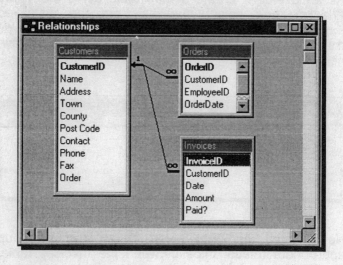

It is important that you should complete this exercise, as it consolidates what we have done so far and, in any case, we will be using all three tables in what comes next. So go ahead and try it.

15. CREATING A QUERY

You create a query so that you can ask questions about the data in your database tables. For example, we could find out whether we have more than one order from the same customer in our Adept database.

To do this, start Access, load **ADEPT 1**, and in the Database window click the Queries tab, followed by the **New** button which opens the New Query dialogue box. Selecting the **Find Duplicates Query Wizard**, displays the following:

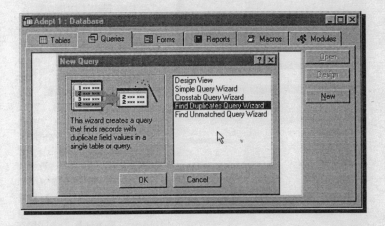

If, on clicking **OK**, Access tells you that this option is not available, then you must close down all running programs, then use the Access SETUP to add the Developer's Tools option to your installation. This can be done easily by placing the first Access distribution disc in the A: drive and using the Windows 95 **Start**, **Run** option, typing **a:\setup** in the displayed dialogue box, and checking the Developer's Tools option.

If the Developer's Tools option is already installed, then the Find Duplicates Query Wizard dialogue box is displayed, as shown on the next page.

From the displayed database tables in this dialogue box, select the Orders table and press the **Next** button.

On the following dialogue box select **CustomerID** as the field you want to check for duplicate values, then press the  button, followed by the **Next** button.

Finally, select the additional fields you would like to see along with the duplicate values, by selecting those you want from the next dialogue box, either one at a time or, if you decide to select all of them, as shown here, by clicking the 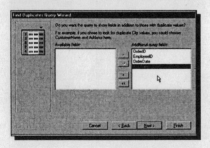 button. Clicking the **Finish** button displays the following Select Query screen.

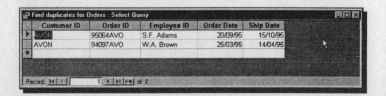

If you examine the original Orders table, you will indeed find that it contains two orders from AVON.

170

Types of Queries

The query we have created so far, is known as the *Select Query*, which is the most common type of query. However, with Access you can also create and use other types of queries, as follows:

- **Crosstab query** - used to present data with row and column headings, just like a spreadsheet. It can be used to summarise large amounts of data in a more readable form.

- **Action query** - used to make changes to many records in one operation. For example, you might like to remove from a given table all records that meet certain criteria, make a new table, or append records to a table. Obviously, this type of query has to be treated with care!

- **Union query** - used to match fields from two or more tables.

- **Pass-through query** - used to pass commands to an SQL (see below) database.

- **Data-definition query** - used to create, change, or delete tables in an Access database using SQL statements.

SQL stands for Structured Query Language, often used to query, update, and manage relational databases. Each query created by Access has an associated SQL statement that defines the action of that query. Thus, if you are familiar with SQL, you can use such statements to view and modify queries, or set form and report properties. However, these actions can be done more easily with the QBE (query-by-example) grid, to be discussed next. If you design union queries, pass-through queries, or data-definition queries, then you must use SQL statements, as these type of queries can not be designed with the QBE grid. Finally, to create a sub-query, you use the QBE grid, but you enter an SQL SELECT statement for criteria, as we shall see in the next QBE grid example.

The Query Window

The Query window is a graphical query-by-example (QBE) tool. Because of Access' graphical features, you can use the mouse to select, drag, and manipulate objects in the query window to define how you would like to see your data.

An example of a ready made Query window can be seen by selecting the Find duplicates for Orders query and clicking the **Design** button on the Database window. This action opens the Select Query dialogue box shown below.

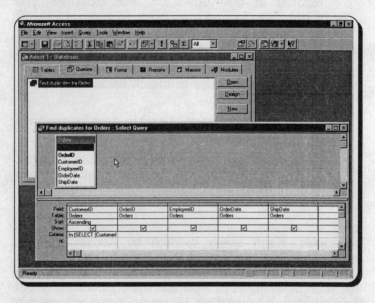

You can add a table to the top half of the Query window by simply dragging the table from the Database window. Similarly, you can add fields to the bottom half of the Query window (the QBE grid) by dragging fields from the tables on the top half of the Query window. In addition, the QBE grid is used to select the sort order of the data, or insert criteria, such as SQL statements.

To see the full SQL SELECT statement written by Access as the criteria selection when we first defined the query, widen the width of the first field, as follows:

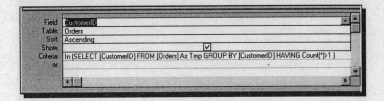

Note the part of the statement which states 'As Tmp GROUP'. Access collects the data you want as a temporary group, called a *dynaset*. This special set of data behaves like a table, but it is not a table; it is a dynamic view of the data from one or more tables, selected and sorted by the particular query.

Creating a New Query:

Below, we show a screen dump created by first clicking the Queries tab, then pressing the **New** button on the Database window. In the displayed New Query dialogue box, select Design View and press the **OK** button. This opens both the Select Query and the Show Table dialogue boxes shown overleaf.

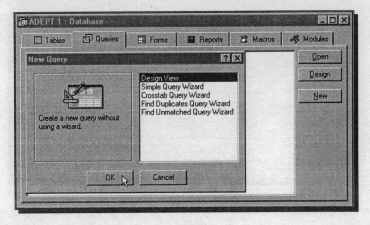

173

The Invoices and Customers tables were then added to the Select Query window, as shown below.

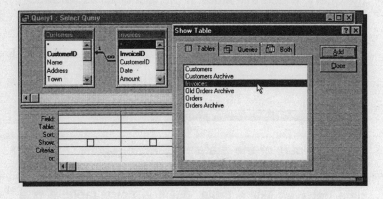

Adding Fields to a Query Window:

Below we show a screen in which the Paid? and InvoiceID fields have been dragged from the Invoices table and added to the Query window. In addition, the Name and Contact fields have been dragged from the Customers table and placed on the Query window, while the Phone field from the Customers table is about to be added to the Query window.

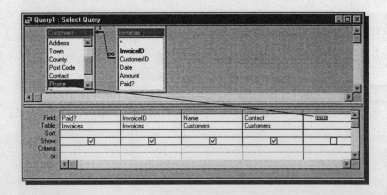

Having dragged all five fields from the two tables onto the QBE grid, we have added the word No as the criteria on the Paid? field and selected Ascending as the Sort for the InvoiceID field.

Note that the Invoices and Customers tables are joined by a line that connects the two CustomerID fields. The join line was created when we designed the tables and their relationships in the previous chapter. Even if you have not created these relationships, Access will join the tables in a query automatically when the tables are added to a query, provided each table has a field with the same name and a compatible data type and one of those fields is a primary key. A primary field is displayed in bold in the Query window.

If you have not created relationships between your tables yourself, or Access has not joined your tables automatically, you can still use related data in your query by joining the tables in the Query window.

Clicking the Run icon on the Toolbar, shown here, instantly displays all the unpaid invoices with the details you have asked for, as follows:

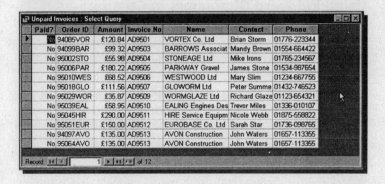

Paid?	Order ID	Amount	Invoice No	Name	Contact	Phone
No	94085VOR	£120.84	AD9501	VORTEX Co. Ltd	Brian Storm	01776-223344
No	94099BAR	£99.32	AD9503	BARROWS Associat	Mandy Brown	01554-664422
No	95002STO	£55.98	AD9504	STONEAGE Ltd	Mike Irons	01765-234567
No	95006PAR	£180.22	AD9505	PARKWAY Gravel	James Stone	01534-987654
No	95010WES	£68.52	AD9506	WESTWOOD Ltd	Mary Slim	01234-667755
No	95018GLO	£111.56	AD9507	GLOWORM Ltd	Peter Summe	01432-746523
No	95029WOR	£35.87	AD9509	WORMGLAZE Ltd	Richard Glaze	01123-654321
No	95039EAL	£58.95	AD9510	EALING Engines Des	Trevor Miles	01336-010107
No	95045HIR	£290.00	AD9511	HIRE Service Equipm	Nicole Webb	01875-558822
No	95051EUR	£150.00	AD9512	EUROBASE Co. Ltd	Sarah Star	01736-098765
No	94097AVO	£135.00	AD9513	AVON Construction	John Waters	01657-113355
No	95064AVO	£135.00	AD9513	AVON Construction	John Waters	01657-113355

Record: 1 of 12

To save your newly created query, use the **File, Save As/Export** command, and give it a name such as 'Unpaid Invoices' in the Save As dialogue box.

Types of Criteria

Access accepts the following expressions as criteria:

Arithmetic Operators		Comparison Operators		Logical Operators	
*	Multiply	<	Less than	And	And
/	Divide	<=	Less than or equal	Or	Inclusive or
+	Add	>	Greater than	Xor	Exclusive or
-	Subtract	>=	Greater than or equal	Not	Not equivalent
		=	Equal	Eqv	Equivalent
		<>	Not equal	Imp	Implication

Other operators		
Between	Between 50 And 150	All values between 50 and 150
In	In("Bath","Bristol")	All records with Bath and Bristol
Is	Is Null	All records with no value in that field
Like	Like "Brian *"	All records with Brian something in field
&	[Name]&" "&[Surname]	Concatenates strings

Using Wildcard Characters in Criteria:

In the previous example we used the criteria A* to mean any company whose name starts with the letter A. The asterisk in this criteria is known as a wildcard character.

To search for a pattern, you can use the asterisk (*) and the question mark (?) as wildcard characters when specifying criteria in expressions. An asterisk stands for any number of characters, while a question mark stands for any single character in the same position as the question mark.

The following examples show the use of wildcard characters in various types of expressions:

176

Entered Expression	Meaning	Examples
a?	Any two-letter word beginning with A	am, an, as, at
???d	Any four-letter word ending with d	find, hand, land yard
Sm?th	Any five-letter word beginning with Sm and ending with th	Smith Smyth
fie*	Any word starting with the letters fie	field, fiend, fierce, fiery
*ght	Any word ending with ght	alight, eight, fight, light, might, sight
*/5/95	All dates in May '95	1/5/95
a	Any word with the letter a in it	Brian, Mary, star, yard

Combining Criteria

By specifying additional criteria in a Query window you can create powerful queries for viewing your data. In the examples below we have added the field Amount to our Unpaid Invoices query.

The AND Criteria with Different Fields: When you insert criteria in several fields, but in the same row, Access assumes that you are searching for records that meet all of the criteria. For example, the criteria below list the records shown on the next page.

Field:	Paid?	Amount	InvoiceID	Name	Contact
Table:	Invoices	Invoices	Invoices	Customers	Customers
Sort:					
Show:	☑	☑	☑	☑	☑
Criteria:	No	Between 50 And 150			Like "M*"
or					

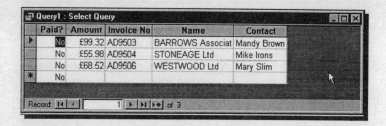

The OR Criteria with the Same Field: If you include multiple criteria in one field only, then Access assumes that you are searching for records that meet any one of the specified criteria. For example, the criteria <50 or >100 in the field Amount, shown below, list the required records, only if the No in the Paid? field is inserted in both rows.

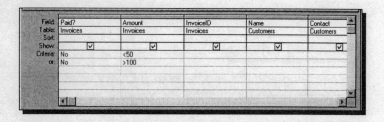

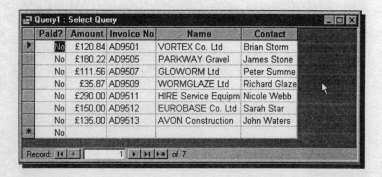

The OR Criteria with Different Fields: If you include
multiple criteria in different fields, but in different rows,
then Access assumes that you are searching for
records that meet either one or the other of the
specified criteria. For example, the criteria Yes in the
Paid? field and the criteria <50 in the Amount field, but
in different rows, list the following records.

Field:	Paid?	Amount	InvoiceID	Name	Contact
Table:	Invoices	Invoices	Invoices	Customers	Customers
Sort:					
Show:	☑	☑	☑	☑	☑
Criteria:	Yes				
or:		<50			

Query1 : Select Query

	Paid?	Amount	Invoice No	Name	Contact
▶	Yes	£103.52	AD9502	AVON Construction	John Waters
	Yes	£123.45	AD9508	SILVERSMITH Co	Adam Smith
	No	£35.87	AD9509	WORMGLAZE Ltd	Richard Glaze
*	No				

Record: ◄◄ ◄ 1 ► ►► ►* of 3

The AND and OR Criteria Together: The following
choice of criteria will cause Access to retrieve either
records that have Yes in the Paid? field and the
company's name starts with the letter A, or records that
the invoice amount is less than £50.

Field:	Paid?	Amount	InvoiceID	Name	Contact
Table:	Invoices	Invoices	Invoices	Customers	Customers
Sort:					
Show:	☑	☑	☑	☑	☑
Criteria:	Yes			Like "A*"	
or:		<50			

179

The retrieved records from such a query are shown below.

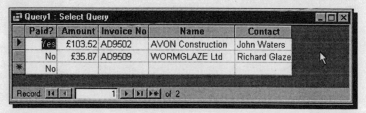

Calculating Totals in Queries:

Access allows you to perform calculations on groups of records. For example, to find the total value of unpaid invoices grouped by month, use the following query.

Functions, such as 'sum', are entered in the Total row of a query which can be displayed by clicking the Totals button, shown here, while in Design View. Note the form of the entry in the third column of the Field row.

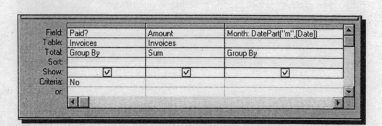

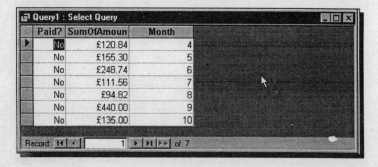

16. USING FORMS & REPORTS

We saw towards the end of Chapter 13 how easy it was to create a single column form to view our Customers table. To see this again, open **ADEPT 1** and in the Database window click the Form tab, then double-click on Form1, which should display the following:

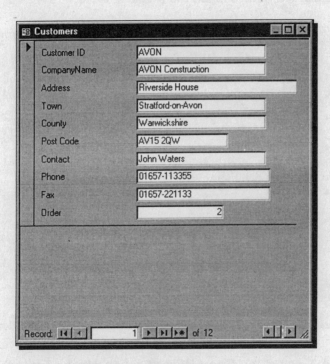

You can use forms to find, edit, and add data in a convenient manner. Access provides you with an easy way of designing various types of forms, some of which are discussed here. Forms look good on screen, but do not produce very good output on paper, whereas reports are designed to look good on paper, but do not necessarily look good on screen.

Using the Form Wizard

Using the Form Wizard, you can easily display data from either a table or a query in form view.

In the Database window, first click the Forms tab, then the **New** button which opens the New Form dialogue box in which you must choose either a table or a query on which to base the new form. In the screen dump below, we have chosen the Invoices table.

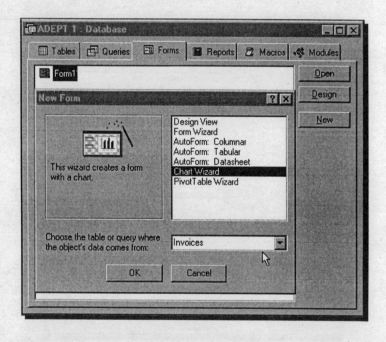

Next, select the **Chart Wizard** option which causes the Form Wizard to display a number of dialogue boxes. As usual, after making appropriate selections, click the **Next** button to progress through the automatic design of the particular form. As you can see from the above screen dump, there are 6 different types of forms available for you to choose from. Their function will be discussed shortly.

To continue with our example, the Wizard displays the following dialogue box in which you are asked to specify the fields that contain the data you want to chart. We chose InvoiceID and Amount.

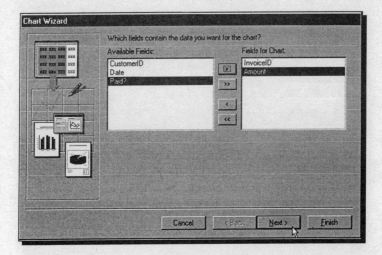

This opens another dialogue box in which you are asked what type of chart you would like. We chose the third one before pressing **Next**.

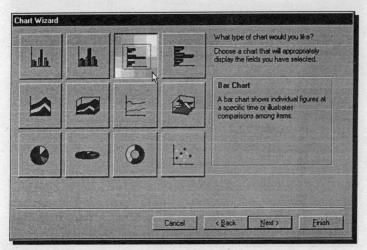

In the following dialogue box, double-click the x-axis button (the one with the caption 'SumOfAmount') and select 'None' from the list in the displayed Summarize dialogue box, shown below, and press **OK**.

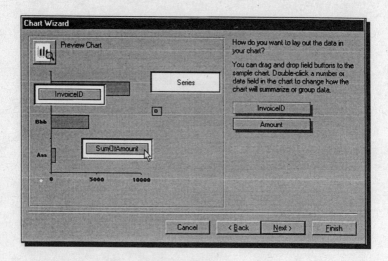

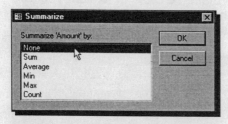

The Wizard then asks you what name you would like to give to this form - we chose to call it 'Invoice Amounts'.

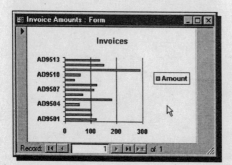

Pressing the **Finish** button, allows the Wizard to display the final result, shown here to the left. It is as easy as that to get a graphical view of the amounts involved in each of your invoices.

The available choice of Form Wizards have the following function:

Type of Form	Function
Design View	Design a form from scratch.
Form Wizard	Automatically creates a form based on the fields you select.
AutoForm: Columnar	Creates a columnar form with all the field labels appearing in the first column and the data in the second. The form displays one record at a time.
AutoForm: Tabular	Tabulates a screen full of records in tabular form with the field labels appearing at the head of each column.
AutoForm: Datasheet	Similar to the Tabular form, but in worksheet display format.
Chart Wizard	Displays data graphically.
PivotTable Wizard	Creates a form with an Excel PivotTable - an interactive table that can summarise a large number of data using the format and calculation methods specified by the user.

Access also allows you to design a form that contains another form. This type of form, called main/subform, allows data from related tables to be viewed at the same time.

Customising a Form:

You can customise a form by changing the appearance of text, data, and any other attributes. To have a look at some of these options, double click on Form1 to display the Customers form, then click the Design View button on the Toolbar.

What appears on your screen is shown below:

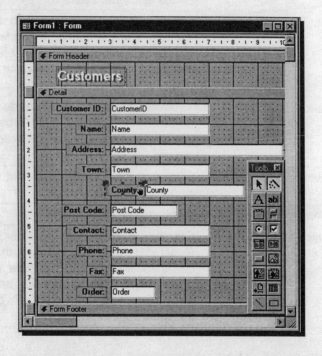

As you can see, a form in Design View is made up of boxes attached to a grid. Clicking at the County box, for example, causes markers to appear around it as shown above. When the mouse pointer is then placed within either the label box or data box, it changes to a hand which indicates that you can drag the box to a new position, as we have done above. This method moves both label and data boxes together.

If you look more closely at the markers around the label and data boxes, you will see that they are of different size, as shown below.

The larger ones are 'move' handles, while the smaller ones are 'size' handles. In the above example you can use the 'move' handles of either the label or the data box to move one independently of the other. The label box can also be sized. To size the data box, click on it so that the markers appear around it.

Boxes on a form can be made larger by simply pointing to the sizing handles and dragging them in the appropriate direction.

In addition to moving and enlarging label and data boxes, you can further customise a form using the various new buttons that appear on the Tool bar when in Design View, shown below in two tiers.

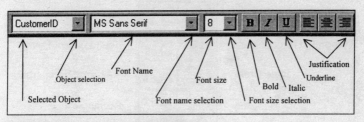

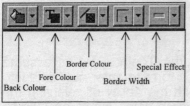

Do try and experiment with moving and sizing label and data boxes and also increasing their font size. If you don't like the result, simply don't save it. Skills gained here will be used in the Report design section.

The Toolbox

The Toolbox can be used either to design a Form or Report from scratch (a task beyond the scope of this book), or to add controls to them, such as a Combo (drop-down) box. The function of each tool on the Toolbox is listed below.

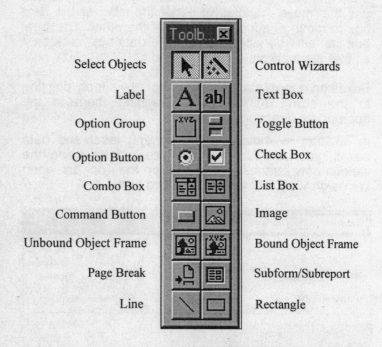

Select Objects	Control Wizards
Label	Text Box
Option Group	Toggle Button
Option Button	Check Box
Combo Box	List Box
Command Button	Image
Unbound Object Frame	Bound Object Frame
Page Break	Subform/Subreport
Line	Rectangle

As an example of using the Toolbox, let us assume that we would like to use a form to enter new data into our Invoices table, but with the ability of selecting the CustomerID field from a drop-down menu - a Combo box.

To achieve the above, execute the following steps:

- On the Database window first click the Forms tab followed by the **New** button.

- In the New Form dialogue box select the **Form Wizard** option, choose Invoices as the table on which to base the new Form, and press the **OK** button.

- In the second dialogue box, select all the fields from the Invoices table, and click the **Next** button.

- In the third dialogue box, select **Columnar** as the preferred form layout, and press **Next**.

- In the fourth dialogue box, select **Standard** as the preferred style for your form and press **Next**.

- In the fifth dialogue box, name your form 'Add Invoices', and press **Finish**. The following form is created and displayed on your screen.

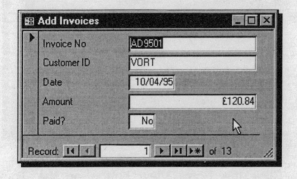

- When the above form appears on the screen, click the Design View button on the Toolbar, and enlarge the Add Invoices form so that both the Header and Footer sections are visible on the form.

- Click the CustomerID field on the form, and delete both its Label and Data boxes by clicking each individually and pressing the <Del> key.

- Click the Combo Box on the Toolbox, and point and click at the area where the CustomerID field used to be on the form.

- In the subsequent dialogue boxes, select options which will cause the Combo Box to look up the values from the Customers table, and from the CustomerID field and store a selected value in the CustomerID field. Specify that the Combo Box should have the label Customer ID:.

- Move and size both the Label and Data boxes of the Combo box into the position shown below.

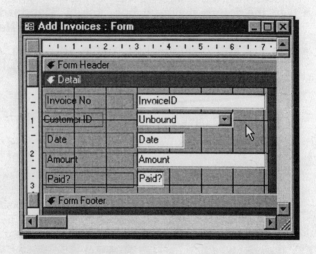

- Click the Form View button on the Toolbar, followed by the New Record button at the bottom of the Add Invoices form, both of which are shown below.

- The entry form should now look as follows:

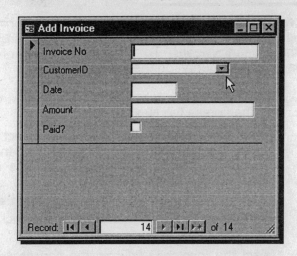

From now on, whenever you want to add a new invoice to the Invoices table, use the Add Invoices form from the Database window, then click the New Record button on either the Toolbar or the Add Invoices form itself to display an empty form. Next, type in the relevant information in the appropriate data boxes on the form, but when you come to fill in the Customer ID field, click instead the down arrow against its data box to display the drop-down menu shown here. Select one of the existing customers on the list, and click the Next Record button at the bottom of the Add Invoices form.

Try the above procedure with the following details:

```
AD9514   WEST      28/10/95      £140
```

then verify that indeed the information has been recorded by double-clicking the Invoices table on the Database window.

Using the Report Wizard

We will use the skills gained in manipulating Forms in Design View to produce an acceptable report created by the Report Wizard. To produce a report of the Unpaid Invoices query, do the following:

- Click the Reports tab on the Database window and then press the **Next** button.

- In the New Report dialogue box, select the **Report Wizard** option, and choose the 'Unpaid Invoices' as the query where the object's data will come from, and press **OK**.

- Select all the fields (except for the Paid? field) which are to appear on your report and click the **Next** button.

- Select the InvoiceID field as the sort field, and accept all subsequent default settings. Call the report 'Unpaid Invoices Report'. The report is created for you as follows:

Unpaid Invoices Report

Invoice No	Order ID	Amount	Name	Contact	Phone
AD9501	94085VOR	£120.84	VORTEX Co. Ltd	Brian Storm	01776-223344
AD9503	84099BAR	£99.32	BARROWS Assoc	Mandy Brown	01554-664422
AD9504	95002STO	£55.98	STONEAGE Ltd	Mike Irons	01765-234567
AD9505	95006PAR	£180.22	PARKWAY Gravel	James Stone	01534-987654
AD9506	95010WES	£68.52	WESTWOOD Ltd	Mary Slim	01234-667755
AD9507	95018GLO	£111.56	GLOWORM Ltd	Peter Summers	01432-746523
AD9509	95029WOR	£35.87	WORMGLAZE Ltd	Richard Glazer	01123-654321
AD9510	95039EAL	£58.95	EALING Engines D	Trevor Miles	01336-010107
AD9511	95045HIR	£290.00	HIRE Service Equi	Nicole Webb	01875-558822
AD9512	95051EUR	£150.00	EUROBASE Co. Lt	Sarah Star	01736-098765
AD9513	94097AVO	£135.00	AVON Constructio	John Waters	01657-113355
AD9513	95064AVO	£135.00	AVON Constructio	John Waters	01657-113355

Obviously this report is not quite acceptable. The problem is mainly the fact that all text fields are left justified within their columns, while numerical fields are right justified.

What we need to do is display it in Design View so that we can change the position of the numeric fields. To do this, use the **View, Toolbars** command, highlight the Report Design item in the **Toolbars** list of the displayed dialogue box, shown here, and press the **Close** button. This displays an additional Toolbar which allows you access to the Design View button. Clicking this button displays the Report as follows:

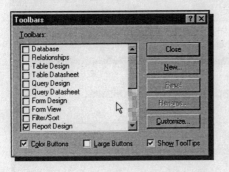

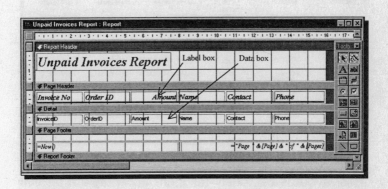

Use the mouse to move the Amount data box to the left, and then right justify the text in the Amount label and data boxes and make them smaller, as shown on the next page.

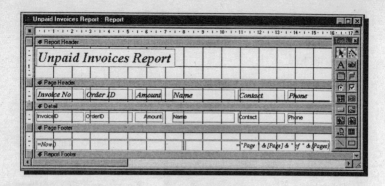

The corresponding report is now as follows:

Unpaid Invoices Report

Invoice No	Order ID	Amount	Name	Contact	Phone
AD9501	94085VOR	£120.84	VORTEX Co. Ltd	Brien Storm	01776-223344
AD9503	94099BAR	£99.32	BARROWS Associates	Mandy Brown	01554-664422
AD9504	95002STO	£55.98	STONEAGE Ltd	Mike Irons	01765-234567
AD9505	95006PAR	£180.22	PARKWAY Gravel	James Stone	01534-987654
AD9506	95010WES	£68.52	WESTWOOD Ltd	Mary Slim	01234-667755
AD9507	95018GLO	£111.56	GLOWORM Ltd	Peter Summers	01432-746523
AD9509	95029WOR	£35.87	WORMGLAZE Ltd	Richard Glazer	01123-654321
AD9510	95039EAL	£58.95	EALING Engines Design	Trevor Miles	01336-010107
AD9511	95045HIR	£290.00	HIRE Service Equipment	Nicole Webb	01875-558822
AD9512	95051EUR	£150.00	EUROBASE Co. Ltd	Sarah Star	01736-098765
AD9513	94097AVO	£135.00	AVON Construction	John Waters	01657-113355
AD9513	95064AVO	£135.00	AVON Construction	John Waters	01657-113355

This layout is obviously far more acceptable than that of the original report created by the Report Wizard.

We hope we have covered enough features of the program in this book to give you the foundations needed to make you want to explore Access more fully by yourselves.

194

17. THE SCHEDULE+ APPLICATION

Schedule+ is a program that lets you organise your time by allowing you to fill in and see at a glance an appointments and meetings diary. This diary can be viewed with a daily, weekly, or monthly format. Switching from one view to another is simply done by clicking at a named tab. The program also allows you to produce 'to do' lists and track projects, as well as build a database of contacts. Schedule+ can be used *online* or *offline*.

To work online, your computer must be connected to a shared network resource, which is imperative if you are planning to use the group-scheduling features of Schedule+. In that case, your computer must have a connection to a *postoffice* which is a list of Mail users on the system. When working online, both your schedule file on the postoffice and your local file are kept up to date.

You work offline if your computer hasn't a connection to postoffice. When working offline, the group-scheduling features of Schedule+ are not available to you, and the copy of your schedule file on the postoffice isn't updated until you connect to the postoffice again.

Whether you work online or offline, Schedule+ ensures the privacy of your personal schedule information by asking you to sign with your mail name and password before it displays your schedule.

If you have upgraded your system to Windows 95 from an earlier version of Windows, and you have had a previous version of MS-Office, then you might find that you have two versions of Schedule+ on your computer. Version 7.0, for Windows 95 is called **schdpl32.exe** and is in the Msoffice\Schedule folder. The earlier version, **schplus.exe**, is in the Windows folder. In the next section we will make use of this information.

Starting the Schedule+ Program

Schedule+ is started in Windows 95 either by clicking the **Start** button then selecting **Program** and clicking on the 'Schedule+' icon on the cascade menu, by clicking any of the three icons 'Making an Appointment', 'Add a Task', or 'Add a Contact' on the Office Shortcut Bar, or by clicking the 'Open a Document' icon on the Office Shortcut Bar and double-clicking on a schedule file. In the latter case the schedule file will be loaded into Schedule+ at the same time.

If you have both versions of Schedule+ on your computer, then clicking the Schedule+ icon on the Old Office Shortcut Bar will activate the earlier version of the program. To remedy this situation, point to the Schedule+ icon and click the right mouse button, then select the **Properties** option from the drop down menu, click the Shortcut tab of the displayed dialogue box and change the information in the **Target** and **Start in** fields to the one shown below.

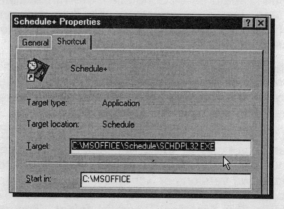

From now on, clicking the Schedule+ icon on the Old Office Shortcut Bar will activate the correct version of Schedule+, thus eliminating a lot of confusion!

The first time you use Schedule+ the program displays its opening screen and asks you for the logon name for the schedule you want to work with, as follows:

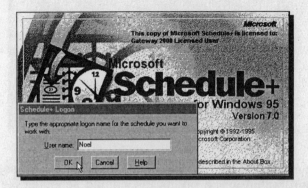

Type a logon name and press the **OK** button. This displays the following screen, in which you select the first option, if you do not have an existing schedule file.

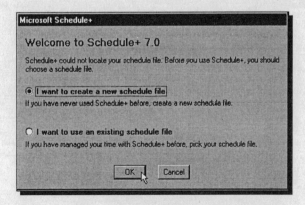

Next, you will be asked to specify where your new schedule file is to be kept (with the Schedule folder as the default), and what the name of the file is going to be, in the following dialogue box.

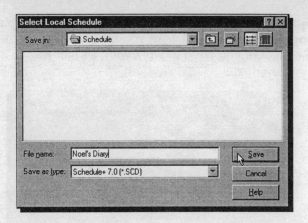

Having typed in the requested information, press the **Save** button which opens the named schedule file, as shown below.

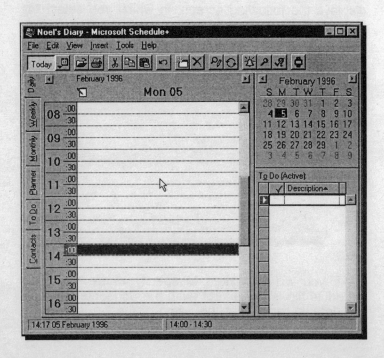

Parts of the Schedule+ Screen

Before we start designing a schedule, let us take a look at the Schedule+ opening screen.

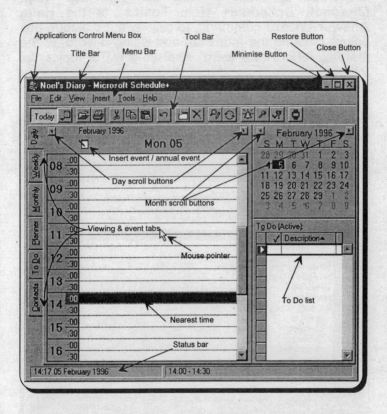

As you can see, this program has some common screen elements with those of other MS-Office applications, even though at first glance it might look radically different.

The central area of this window (the one with the mouse pointer in it) changes the way it displays according to which viewing or event tab is active.

Using Help in Schedule+

The Schedule+ Help Program provides on-line help in the same way as the Help programs of the other MS-Office applications. You can use the **Help, Microsoft Schedule+ Help Topics**, or the **Help, Answer Wizard** command, to display the dialogue box below. Clicking the Index tab and typing a word, or the first few letters of a word, displays a list of topics, as follows:

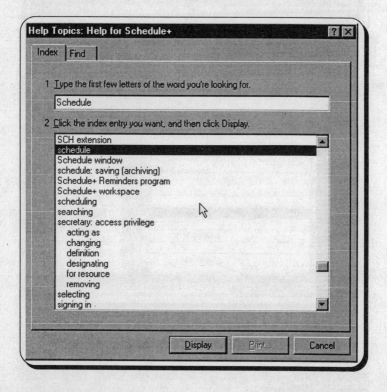

Selecting a topic from the above list and pressing the **Display** button, produces a list of topics found for you to choose from. Help topics can be printed on paper by selecting the topic, then clicking the **Print** button.

The help available in this way is very limited. However, when you choose a topic (any topic will do), press **Display,** then use the **File, Open** command and choose C:\Msoffice\Schedule, select the Schedplus.hlp file and press the **Open** button.

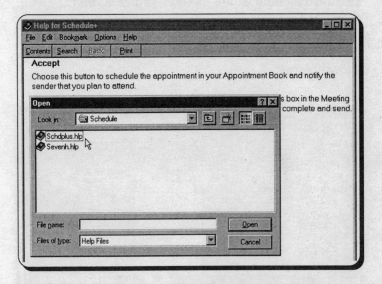

This gives you the usual Help facilities available to all the other MS-Office applications, as shown below.

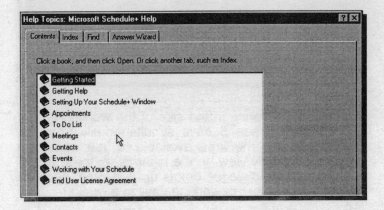

Viewing Appointments

When in Daily view, apart from using the scroll buttons (the ones below the Toolbar) to look at another day, you can click the day you want to look at within the monthly calendar at the top right of the screen.

You also have a choice of the number of days you see at any one time by selecting the **View, Number of Days** command and clicking the required days, as shown below.

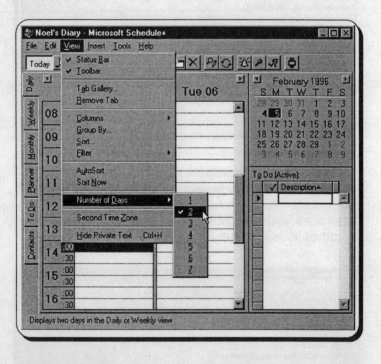

There is a difference in the size of the working area if you choose to see 5 days simultaneously from the Daily view, and the area available to you when you select the Weekly view. In the latter case, the whole of the width of the dialogue box is divided into 5 sections (the default number of working days in a week).

Clicking the Monthly tab, displays a typical monthly diary, as shown below - you might need to widen the monthly window to see all the days of the month at the same time.

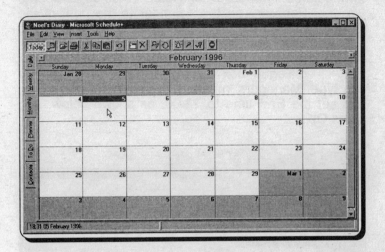

Changing the month you are viewing could not be simpler; just click the scroll buttons under the Toolbar - clicking the left scroll button displays earlier months, while clicking the right scroll button displays later months.

Appointments can be viewed in Schedule+ in several ways, depending on the details you need to know. In the Daily and Weekly view, you can see the date, time, and the description of an appointment. You also have the facility to use symbols to indicate whether the appointment is recurring, tentative, or private, and whether a reminder has been set or other users have been invited (these will be discussed next).

Information relevant to an appointment, such as location, who attends, etc., is also displayed in the Appointment dialogue box.

Entering Appointments

To start with, let us type in two appointments for meetings; one for 10:00 a.m. on 8 February, the other for the same time four weeks later. To do so, click on 8 February on the calendar to the right of the entry area, move the cursor to 10:00 a.m. and click the Make a New Appointment icon, shown here. This opens the Appointment dialogue box displayed below in which you can type 'Managers' meeting' in the **Description** box, and set the **End** time to 12.00, as shown below, and press **OK**.

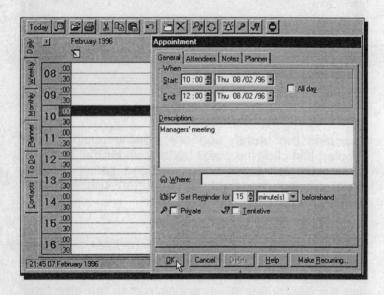

Note that after pressing **OK**, the Reminder icon (the bell) on the Toolbar becomes depressed, and it also appears against the appointment in the entry area. This is because the **Set Reminder** box at the bottom of the Appointment dialogue box is checked.

If you want to make any changes to the newly created appointment, point to it and right-click it.

You can use the options on this drop-down menu to edit, delete, move, or make the appointment recurring. Choosing the last option, opens the Appointment Series dialogue box where you can make the recurring period to 4 weeks, then click the **Until** box to allow you to limit the recurrence of this event.

You can use the Attendees tab on the dialogue box to insert details of who is to attend these meetings, and/or the Notes tab to scribble some information relating to the event.

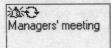

Finally, pressing the **OK** button, causes the recurring symbol to also appear on the appointment entry.

Next, let us assume that you also have a special lunch appointment with your mother on the same day, but four weeks later, as it is her birthday. To enter this information click on 7 March on the calendar to the right of the Daily entry area, and create a yearly appointment 'Lunch with mother' for 1:00 p.m., for 1½ hours, as shown below. Add as notes the reminder 'Birthday lunch'.

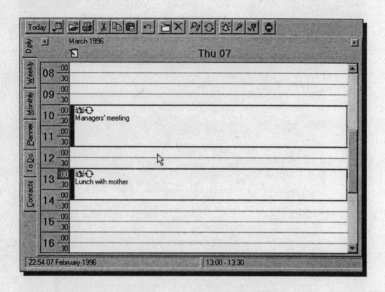

Note that the Managers' meeting is also shown on the same day, as it is four weeks since the last meeting. This information also appears on the Weekly and the Monthly view. Try it!

Printing Information:

Information held in a diary can be printed on paper. Simply use the **File, Print** command and select an appropriate item from the **Print Layout** list displayed in the Print dialogue box. However, before committing anything to paper, use the **Preview** button and save a few trees!

Below we show a preview of the 'Daily - fixed' layout.

Noel's Diary			S	M	T	W	T	F	S
								1	2
Events for 07 March 1996:			3	4	5	6	7	8	9
			10	11	12	13	14	15	16
			17	18	19	20	21	22	23
			24	25	26	27	28	29	30
			31						

Time		Other appointments:
08:00		
:30		
09:00		
:30		
10:00	Managers' meeting	
:30		
11:00		
:30		
12:00		
:30		Task (Active):
13:00	Lunch with mother	
:30		
14:00		
:30		
15:00		
:30		
16:00		
:30		

Other Schedule+ Facilities

Apart from the 'Appointment Book', Schedule+ contains all the other elements needed to give you an effective time-management tool. These elements are accessed by appropriate tabs situated on the left edge of the screen. Each tab includes one or more of the following:

Planner:

If you are using Microsoft Mail and are connected to a mail server, you can organise meetings and send requests to participants and then track the status of their response. You can even give other Schedule+ users permissions to view your diary and to plan meetings with you at times which are not so busy, but at the same time be able to maintain private information in your diary.

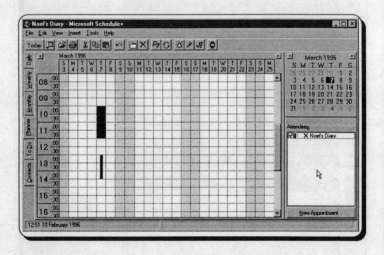

From the Planner, you can create a list of participants, select a time for the meeting, and create the meeting requests. You can also set up a meeting from any view by using the Meeting Wizard.

To Do List:

Tasks appear in the 'To Do List', which you can either display on a separate tab or with other elements, such as the Daily view of the Appointment Book.

Below we show two groups of tasks, one entitled 'Info', the other 'Upgrades', with 'None' being the default. Within each group you can set priorities which cause the list to sort itself automatically according to priority. You can also set the date by which a task has to be completed and its duration.

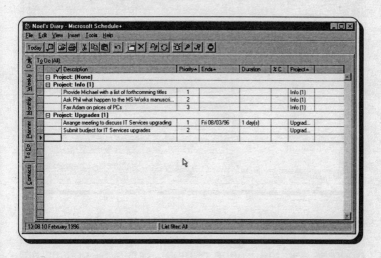

Note the small square box to the left of the project name. In the above display this is marked with a minus sign. Clicking on this square hides all the entries under this project title and displays a plus sign in the small box. To delete a task, click the selection button on the left of an entry to highlight it and press the <Del> key.

The amount of information displayed in the list can be controlled by you, including filtering, grouping, and sorting of the various items. All information relevant to a task is also displayed in the Task dialogue box.

Contacts:

The Contacts tab displays your contacts in a combined business card and list view. You can also add the Contact List tab in a list, or you can add one of the tabs that combines your Contact List view with another view, such as your Planner, with full control over the amount of information displayed.

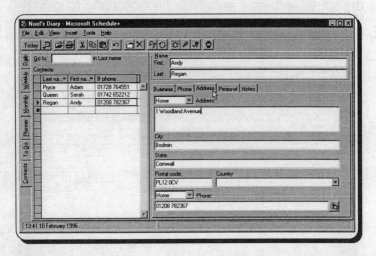

In the contacts entry list shown above, we have chosen to enter information in the Home option for both the Address and the Phone number. Business options are also available.

All information relevant to a contact is also displayed in the Contact dialogue box.

 If you have a modem and it is connected to a telephone line, you can get your computer to ring a selected number by simply clicking the Dial Phone icon, shown here, which appears to the extreme right of the Phone entry box.

Finally, it might be worth your while to look at the **Seven Habits Help Topics** under **Help**, which discuss the implementation of personal organisation habits.

18. SHARING INFORMATION

You can link or embed all or part of an existing file created either in an Office application or in any other application that supports Object Linking and Embedding (OLE). However, if an application does not support OLE, then you must use the copy/cut and paste commands to copy or move information from one application to another.

In general, you copy, move, link or embed information depending on the imposed situation, as follows:

Imposed Situation	Method to Adopt
Inserted information will not need updating, or Application does not support OLE.	Copy or move
Inserted information needs to be automatically updated in the destination file as changes are made to the data in the source file, or Source file will always be available and you want to minimise the size of the destination file, or Source file is to be shared amongst several users.	Link
Inserted information might need to be updated but source file might not be always accessible, or Destination files needs to be edited without having these changes reflected in the source file.	Embed

Copying or Moving Information

To copy or move information between programs running under Windows, such as Microsoft applications, is extremely easy. To move information, use the drag and drop facility, while to copy information, use the **Edit, Copy** and **Edit, Paste** commands.

To illustrate the technique, we will copy the file PROJECT3.XLS created in Excel into Word. We will consider the following two possibilities:

Source File Available without Application:

Let us assume that you only have the source file PROJECT3.XLS on disc, but not the application that created it (that is you don't have Excel). In such a situation, you can only copy the contents of the whole file to the destination (in our case Word). To achieve this, do the following:

- Start Word and minimise it on the Taskbar.

- Use My Computer (or Explorer) to locate the file whose contents you want to copy into Word.

- Click the filename that you want to copy, hold the mouse button down and point to Word on the Taskbar until the application opens.

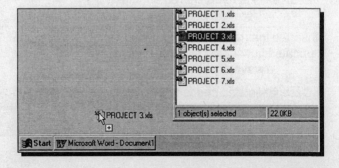

- While still holding the mouse button down, move the mouse pointer into Word's open document to the exact point where you would like to insert the contents of PROJECT3.XLS.

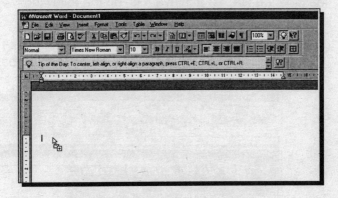

- Release the mouse button to place the contents of PROJECT3.XLS into Word at that point.

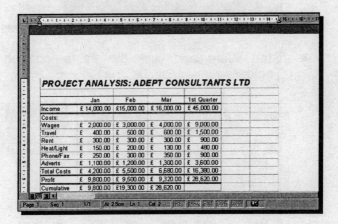

Source File and Application Available:

Assuming that you have both the file and the application that created it on your computer, you can copy all or part of the contents of the source file to the destination file. To achieve this, do the following:

- Start Excel and open PROJECT3.XLS.

- Highlight as much information as you would like to copy and click the copy icon on the Toolbar.

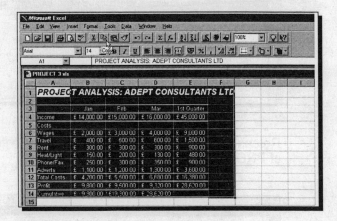

- Start Word and click the Paste icon on the Toolbar.

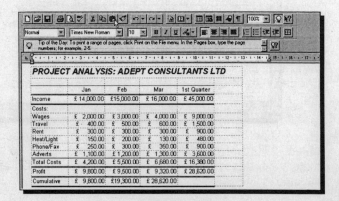

Object Linking and Embedding

Object Linking is copying information from one file (the source file) to another file (the destination file) and maintaining a connection between the two files. When information in the source file is changed, then the information in the destination file is automatically updated. Linked data is stored in the source file, while the file into which you place the data stores only the location of the source and displays a representation of the linked data.

For example, you would use Object Linking if you would want an Excel chart included in, say, a Word document to be updated whenever you changed the information used to create the chart in the first place within Excel. In such a case, the Excel worksheet containing the chart would be referred to as the source file, while the Word document would be referred to as the destination file.

Object Embedding is inserting information created in one file (the source file) into another file (the container file). After such information has been embedded, the object becomes part of the container file. When you double-click an embedded object, it opens in the application in which it was created in the first place. You can then edit it in place, and the original object in the source application remains unchanged.

Thus, the main differences between linking and embedding are where the data is stored and how it is updated after you place it in your file. Linking saves you disc space as only one copy of the linked object is kept on disc. Embedding a logo chosen for your headed paper, saves the logo with every saved letter!

In what follows, we will discuss how you can link or embed either an entire file or selected information from an existing file, and how you can edit an embedded object. Furthermore, we will examine how to mail merge a letter written in Word with a list created either in Access, Excel, Schedule+, or even Word itself.

Embedding a New Object:

To embed a new object into an application, do the following:

- Open the container file, say Word, and click where you want to embed the new object.

- Use the **Insert, Object** command, to open the Object dialogue box, shown below, when the **Create New** tab is clicked.

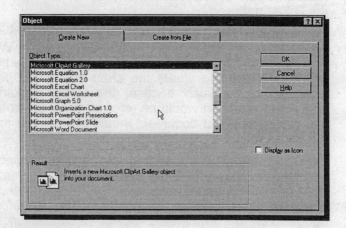

Note that only applications which are installed on your computer and support linking and embedding appear in the **Object Type** box.

- In the **Object Type** box, click the type of object you want to create, and press **OK**.

As an example, we selected Microsoft ClipArt (you could select a different application) which opens the Microsoft ClipArt Gallery from which we selected the object shown here. Pressing the **Insert** button on the ClipArt application, embeds the object within Word. Double-clicking on such an object, opens up the original application.

216

Linking or Embedding an Existing File:

To embed an existing file in its entirety into another application, do the following:

- Open the container file, say Word, and click where you want to embed the file.

- Use the **Insert, Object** command, to open the Object dialogue box, shown below, when the **Create from File** tab is clicked.

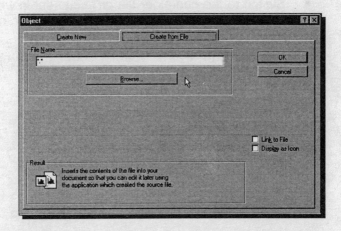

To locate the file you want to link or embed, click **Browse**, and then select the options you want.

- In the **File Name** box, type the name of the file you want to link or embed.

- To maintain a link to the original file, check the **Link to File** box.

Note: To insert graphics files, use the **Insert, Picture** command instead of the **Insert, Object** command. This opens up the Insert Picture dialogue box which allows you to specify within a **Look in** box the folder and file you want to insert.

Linking or Embedding Selected Information:

To link or embed selected information from an existing file created in one application into another, do the following:

- Select the information in the source file you want to link or embed.

- Use the **Edit, Copy** command to copy the selected information to the Clipboard.

- Switch to the container file or document in which you want to place the information, and then click where you want the information to appear.

- Use the **Edit, Paste Special** command to open the following dialogue box:

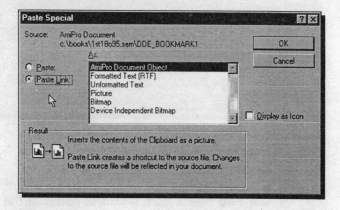

- To link the information, click the **Paste Link** radio button, or to embed the information, click the **Paste** radio button. In the **As** box, click the item with the word 'Object' in its name. For example, if you copied the information from an AmiPro document, as we have for this example, the AmiPro Document Object appears in the **As** box. Select this object and press **OK**.

Linking or Embedding into Access:

When you link or embed an object in a Microsoft Access form or report, the object is displayed in an object frame. To illustrate this point, start Access, select the Forms tab, and open Form1, which we created in Chapter 13. Then do the following:

- Switch to Design View, then use the **Insert, Object** command which displays the Insert Object dialogue box.

- Select the source application from the **Object Type** list (we have selected the Microsoft ClipArt Gallery), and press **OK**.

- Select the object and press **Insert**. This inserts the object into an unbound frame.

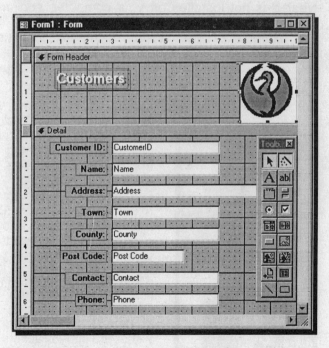

If the object you are embedding is from an Access table, use a bound object frame.

Editing an Embedded Object:

If the application in which you created an embedded object is installed on your computer, double-click the object to open it for editing. Some applications start the original application in a separate window and then open the object for editing, while other applications temporarily replace the menus and toolbars in the current application so that you can edit the embedded object in place, without switching to another window.

To edit an embedded object which was inserted into a Microsoft Access form or report, first switch to Design View, then double-click the object to open the application on which it was created.

If the application in which an embedded object was created is not installed on your computer, convert the object to the file format of an application you do have. For example, if your Word document contains an embedded Microsoft Works Spreadsheet object and you do not have Works, you can convert the object to an Excel Workbook format and edit it in Excel.

Some embedded objects, such as sound and video clips, when double-clicked start playing their contents, instead of opening an application for editing. For example, copying the Goodtime video icon from its folder in the Windows 95 CD into Word and double-clicking the icon, starts the video, as shown here.

To edit one of these objects, select it and use the **Edit, {Video Clip} Object, Edit** command. What appears within the curly brackets here depends on the selected object; video clip in this case.

Mail Merging Lists

There are times when you may want to send the same basic letter to several different people, or companies. The easiest way to do this is with a Merge operation. Two files are prepared; a 'Data' file with the names and addresses, and a 'Form' file, containing the text and format of the letter. The two files are then merged together to produce a third file containing an individual letter to each party listed in the original data file.

Before creating a list of names and addresses for a mail merge, you need to select the Office application that is most suited to the task. For a mail merge, you can use a list you create in Access, Excel, Schedule+, or Microsoft Word.

- For a long list in which you expect to add, change, or delete records, and for which you want a powerful sorting and searching capabilities to your disposal, you should use either Access or Excel, then specify the appropriate data file in the Word Mail Merge Helper (see below).

- To use the list of names and addresses in your Schedule+ Contact List, you select this list in the Word Mail Merge Helper.

- For a small to medium size list of names and addresses in which you do not expect to make many changes, you could select to create a list in the Word Mail Merge Helper.

The Word Mail Merger Helper is a dialogue box in which you specify:

(a) whether you want to create form letters, labels, or print envelopes, (b) where your list of names and addresses (data) is to be found, and (c) what query options are to be applied to your data list before the merging process starts.

These will be explained next with illustrated examples.

We will illustrate the merge procedure by using a memo created in Word (**PCUSERS 1**) and a table which can be created in Word, or already exists either in an electronic book such as Schedule+, in Excel or in an Access table such as Customers in **ADEPT 1**.

No matter which method you choose, first start Word and open the **PCUSERS 1** memo (or your own letter), then provide two empty lines at the very top of the memo/letter by placing the insertion pointer at the beginning of the memo and pressing <Enter> twice. Then select these two empty lines and choose the Normal paragraph style.

Next, select **Tools, Mail Merge** which displays the Mail Merge Helper dialogue box shown below.

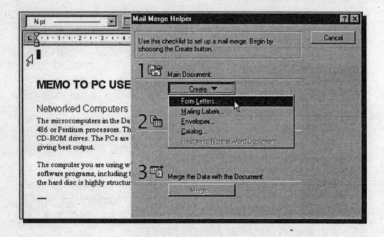

In this box, you define in three successive steps:

1. The document to be used,
2. The source of your data, and
3. The merging of the two.

Start by clicking the **Create** button, select the **Form Letters** option, and click the **Active Window** button.

Next, click the **Get Data** button which causes a drop-down menu to display, shown below.

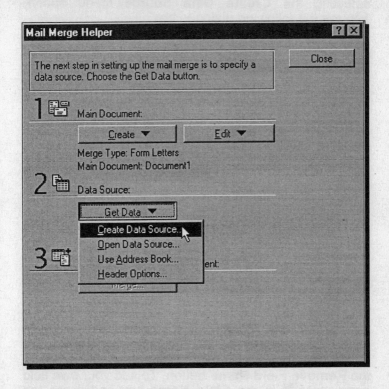

It is from this menu that you can select either to create your data source (the list of addresses) in Word, open (or import) an existing list of addresses which might be found in either Word, Excel, Access, etc., or use a list of contacts in an electronic address book such as Schedule+.

In what follows, we will examine each of these options (in the same order as the list in the above drop-down menu). You can, of course, skip the Create an Address List in Word section, if you already have an existing data list.

Creating an Address List in Word:

Selecting the **Create Data Source** menu option, displays the following dialogue box.

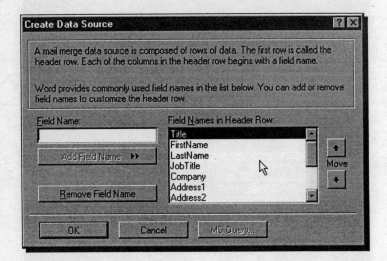

As you can see, Word provides commonly used field names for your address list. Unwanted field names can be deleted from the list by selecting them and pressing the **Remove Field Name** button. To add your own field name, type it in the **Field Name** box and press the **Add Field Name** button. The **Move** buttons to the right of the list can be used to move a selected field in the list to the top or bottom of the list by pressing the up-arrow or down-arrow, respectively.

Having compiled the required field names for your list, pressing the **OK** button, displays a Save As dialogue box, in which you can name your data list, say **Address**. Word automatically adds the file extension **.doc**, and displays the following warning dialogue box which allows you to either edit the data source or the main document.

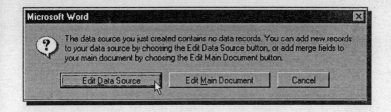

Press the **Edit Data Source** button if you want to create or edit your data list. Doing so displays the following Data Form dialogue box.

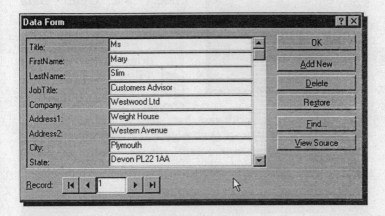

Here you can create a new data list or edit an existing one. We have typed in one fictitious entry in order to demonstrate the process, but we have not attempted to change the field names provided in any way whatsoever.

Having created a Word data list, added to one or edited one, pressing **OK** prompts you to save your changes to the already existing filename.

What follows is common to all existing data files, no matter in which application you chose to create it.

Getting an Address List:

If you have not done so already, open the letter you want to mail merge, place the cursor in the position you want the address to appear, and select **Tools, Mail Merge** in Word. Then press the **Create** button in the Mail Merge Helper and choose **Form Letters**, **Active Window**.

Next, click the **Get Data** button (the 2nd step in the Mail Merge Helper) which causes a drop-down menu, shown here, to display.

Select the **Open Data Source** option, and in the displayed dialogue box, select the drive, and click the down-arrow on the **List Files of Type** box. From here you can choose the type of file that holds your address list, which could be one created in Word or a text editor (or exported in that form from another application), or an Access or Excel file.

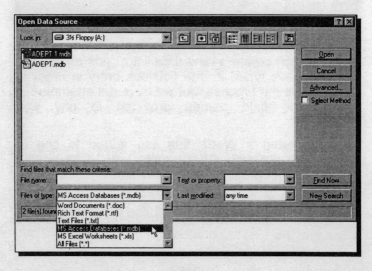

For our example we chose the **MS Access Database** type of file, which lists the databases on the specified drive and path. Next, select the database that holds your address data (in this case **adept 1.mdb**) and click the **OK** button. Access is then loaded and the tables within the selected database are listed, as shown below.

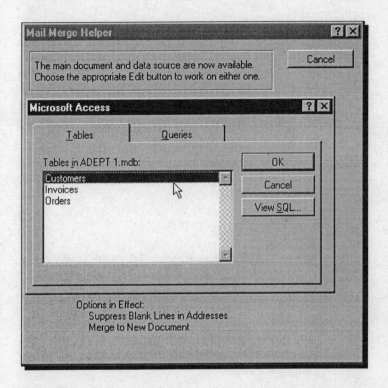

Microsoft Access then asks you to choose the Table that contains your data. In this case, select Customers and click the **OK** button.

Microsoft Word now displays a warning message, shown overleaf, to the effect that no merge fields have been found on your document.

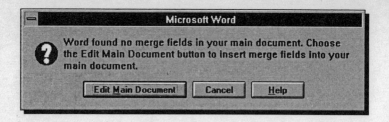

Don't worry about this, as we will rectify this omission, as follows:

- Click the **Edit Main Document** button on the above warning box which displays your document with an additional toolbar below the Formatting bar , as follows:

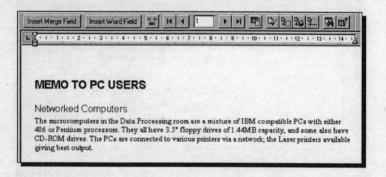

- Click the **Insert Merge Field** button on the new toolbar. This displays the fields in your Customers table.

- Select in turn, Name, Address, Town, County, and Post_Code. The first three are placed on the document on separate lines (by pressing <Enter> after each selection), while the last two are placed on the same line, but separated by a space. Finally, type on a new line the letters FAO: plus a space, and place the Contact field against it.

The first few lines of your document should now look as follows:

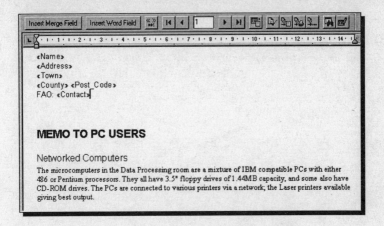

- Click the View Merged Data icon, shown to the right, to see your merged data. Clicking this icon once more, returns you to the screen above so that you can edit your work, or add merge fields.

- Click either the Merge to New Document icon or the Merge to Printer icon to create a new merged document to file or send the merged document to the printer.

That's all there is to it. You will possibly find it takes as little time to do, as it did to read about it!

19. GLOSSARY OF TERMS

Application

Software (program) de-
signed to carry out certain
activity, such as word processing.

Association

An identification of a filename extension to a pro-
gram. This lets Windows
open the program when its
files are selected.

ASCII

A binary code representa-
tion of a character set. The
name stands for 'American
Standard Code for Information Interchange'.

Backup

To make a back-up copy of
a file or a disc for safe-
keeping.

Baud

The unit of measurement
used to describe data trans-
mission speed. One baud is
one bit per second.

Bit

A binary digit; the smallest
unit of information that can
be stored, either as 1 or as
0 (zero).

Bitmap

A technique for managing
the image displayed on a
computer screen.

Browse

A button in some dialogue
boxes that lets you view a
list of files and folders before you make a selection.

Byte	A grouping of binary digits (0 or 1) which represent information.
Card	A removable printed-circuit board that is plugged into a computer expansion slot.
CD-ROM	A device which when installed on your PC, allows the use of CDs.
Cell	The intersection of a column and row in a spreadsheet, or database, which can hold an expression, a label or a number.
Check box	A small box in a dialogue box that can be selected (✓), or cleared (empty).
Click	To quickly press and release a mouse button.
Client application	A Windows application that can accept linked, or embedded, objects.
Clipboard	A temporary storage area of memory, where text and graphics are stored with the cut and copy actions.
Close	To remove a dialogue box or window, or to exit a program.
Command	An instruction given to a computer to carry out a particular action.
CPU	The Central Processing Unit; the main chip that executes all instructions entered into a computer.

Cursor	The blinking line indicating where the next input can be entered.
Database	A collection of related information or data, organised for a specific theme in one or more tables.
DDE	Dynamic data exchange - a process that enables you to exchange data between two or more Windows programs.
Default	The command, device or option automatically chosen by the system.
Desktop	The Windows screen working background, on which you place icons, folders, etc.
Dialogue box	A window displayed on the screen to allow the user to enter information.
Dimmed	Unavailable menu options shown in a different colour.
Disc	A device on which you can store programs and data.
Disc file	A collection of program code, or data, that is stored under a given name on a disc.
Disconnect	To detach a drive, port, or computer from a shared device.
Document	A file produced by an application program.

Domain	A group of devices, servers and computers on a network.
DOS	Disc Operating System; a collection of small specialised programs that allow interaction between user and computer.
Double-click	To quickly press and release a mouse button twice.
DPI	Dots Per Inch; a resolution standard for laser printers.
Drag	To press and hold down the left mouse button while moving the mouse, to move an object on the screen.
Drive name	The letter (followed by a colon) which identifies a floppy disc drive, a hard disc drive, or a CD-ROM drive.
Embedded object	Information in a document that is 'copied' from its source application. Selecting the object opens the creating application from within the document.
Enter key	The key that is pressed after entering data on the command line.
Field	A single column of information of the same type.
File	The name given to an area on disc containing a program or data.

File extension	The optional three-letter suffix following the period in a filename. Windows 95 uses the extension to identify the filetype.
File list	A list of filenames contained in the active directory.
Filename	The name given to a file. In Windows 95 this can be up to 255 characters long.
Filespec	File specification made up of drive, path and filename.
Fixed disc	The hard disc of a computer.
Floppy disc	A removable disc on which information can be stored magnetically. The two main types are a 5¼" flexible disc, and a 3½" stiff disc.
Folder	An area on disc where information relating to a group of files is kept.
Font	A graphic design representing a set of characters, numbers and symbols.
Formatting	The process of preparing a disc so that it can store information.
Function	A built-in formula which performs specific calculations in a spreadsheet or database cell.
Function key	One of the series of 10 or 12 keys marked with the letter F and a numeral, used for specific operations.

235

Graphics card	A device that controls the display on the monitor and other allied functions.
GUI	A Graphic User Interface, such as Windows 95, which uses visual displays to eliminate the need for typing commands.
Hardcopy	Output on paper.
Hard disc	A device built into the computer for holding programs and data. It is sometimes referred to as a fixed disc.
Hardware	The equipment that makes up a computer system, excluding the programs or software.
Help	A Windows system that gives you instructions and additional information.
Highlight	The change to a reverse-video appearance when a menu item or area of text is selected.
Icon	A small graphic image that represents a function or object. Clicking on an icon produces an action.
Insertion point	A flashing bar that shows where typed text will be entered into a document.
Interface	A device that allows you to connect a computer to its peripherals.

236

Key combination	When two or more keys are pressed simultaneously, such as \<Ctrl+Esc>.
Kilobyte	(KB); 1024 bytes of information or storage space.
LAN	Local Area Network; PCs, workstations or minis sharing files and peripherals within the same site.
Linked object	A placeholder for an object inserted into a destination document.
Local	A resource that is located on your computer, not linked to it over a network.
Log on	To gain access to a network.
Long filename	In Windows 95 the name given to a file can be up to 255 characters long.
MCI	Media Control Interface - a standard for files and multimedia devices.
Megabyte	(MB); 1024 kilobytes of information or storage space.
Megahertz	(MHz); Speed of processor in millions of cycles per second.
Memory	Part of computer consisting of storage elements organised into addressable locations that can hold data and instructions.
Menu	A list of available options in an application.

237

Menu bar	The horizontal bar that lists the names of menus.
Microprocessor	The calculating chip within a computer.
MIDI	Musical Instrument Digital Interface - enables devices to transmit and receive sound and music messages.
Monitor	The display device connected to your PC.
Mouse	A device used to manipulate a pointer around your display and activate a certain process by pressing a button.
Multi-tasking	Performing more than one operation at the same time.
Network server	Central computer which stores files for several linked computers.
Operating System	A group of programs that translates your commands to the computer.
Password	A unique character string used to gain access to a network, or an application document.
PATH	The location of a file in the directory tree.
PCX	A standard file format used for bitmapped graphics.
Peripheral	Any device attached to a PC.

Pixel	A picture element on screen; the smallest element that can be independently assigned colour and intensity.
Port	An input/output address through which your PC interacts with external devices.
Print queue	The list of print jobs waiting to be sent to a printer.
Program	A set of instructions which cause the computer to perform certain tasks.
Protocol	It defines the way in which data is transferred over a network.
Processor	The electronic device which performs calculations.
RAM	Random Access Memory. The micro's volatile memory. Data held in it is lost when power is switched off.
Record	A row of information in a table relating to a single entry and comprising one or more fields.
Resource	A directory, or printer, that can be shared over a network.
ROM	Read Only Memory. A PC's non-volatile memory. Data is written into this memory at manufacture and is not affected by power loss.

Scroll bar	A bar that appears at the right side or bottom edge of a window.
Server	A networked computer that is used to share resources.
Shared resource	Any device, program or file that is available to network users.
Software	The programs and instructions that control your PC.
Spreadsheet	An electronic page made of a matrix of rows and columns.
SVGA	Super Video Graphics Array; it has all the VGA modes but with 256 colours.
Table	A two-dimensional structure in which data is stored, like in a speadsheet.
Template	A file blank you can create to contain common text and formatting to use as a basis for new documents.
Text file	An unformatted file of text characters saved in ASCII format.
Tool	Microsoft Office application, such as the word processor or spreadsheet.
Toolbar	A bar containing icons giving quick access to commands.
Toggle	To turn an action on and off with the same switch.

TrueType fonts	Fonts that can be scaled to any size and print as they show on the screen.
VGA	Video Graphics Array; has all modes of EGA, but with 16 colours.
Wildcard character	A character that can be included in a filename to indicate any other character (?) or group of characters (*).
Windows 95	The graphical operating system under which this version of Microsoft Office is installed.

INDEX

NOTES

NOTES

NOTES

COMPANION DISCS TO BOOKS

COMPANION DISCS are available for most books written by the same author(s) and published by BERNARD BABANI (publishing) LTD, as listed at the front of this book (except for those marked with an asterisk). These books contain many pages of file/program listings. There is no reason why you should spend hours typing them into your computer, unless you wish to do so, or need the practice.

COMPANION DISCS come in 3½" format with all example listings.

ORDERING INSTRUCTIONS

To obtain your copy of a companion disc, fill in the order form below or a copy of it, enclose a cheque (payable to **P.R.M. Oliver**) or a postal order, and send it to the address below. Make sure you fill in your name and address and specify the book number and title in your order.

Book No.	Book Name	Unit Price	Total Price
BP		£3.50	
BP		£3.50	
BP		£3.50	
Name .... Address:		Sub-total	£.............
		P & P (@ 45p/disc)	£.............
		Total Due	£.............
Send to: P.R.M. Oliver, CSM, Pool, Redruth, Cornwall, TR15 3SE			

PLEASE NOTE

The author(s) are fully responsible for providing this Companion Disc service. The publishers of this book accept no responsibility for the supply, quality, or magnetic contents of the disc, or in respect of any damage, or injury that might be suffered or caused by its use.